Till Fish Us Do Part

Till
Fish
Us
Do
Part

The Confessions of

a Fisherman's Wife, by

Beatrice Cook

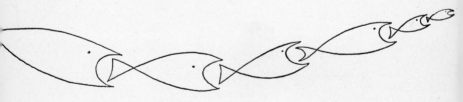

New York 1949, William Morrow & Co., Publishers

Published April, 1949
Second Printing May, 1949

Copyright 1949 by Beatrice Gray Cook.
Printed in the United States of America.
All rights reserved.
Published simultaneously in the Dominion of Canada
by Wm. Collins Sons & Co. Canada Ltd.
* f j l *

To our friends in the San Juan Islands, especially Cappy Bell.

Chapters

1. *A worm's-eye view of fishermen* *11*

2. *All his worldly goods . . .* *22*

3. *"I ain't takin' no women"* *35*

4. *Babies, bottles and bass* *67*

5. *The one that got away* *98*

6. *The king is dead* *125*

7. *Ethan Allen of Waldron Island* *149*

8. *Hook, line, and stinker* *182*

9. *Opening day is a double-header* *203*

10. *Till fish us do part* *228*

Till Fish Us Do Part

A worm's-eye view of fishermen

I am a fishwife—or so it seems after being married over twenty years to a fishin' fool. I married one and raised two and claim to know more about fishermen than a salmon does, which is saying a lot, for fish are smarter than high school girls. I've shared a fisherman's life and therefore know the extremes of unreasonable exultation or blackest despair.

At the altar, I little realized I was pledged to love, honor, and obey three outboard motors, the ways of the river, the whims of the tide, and the wiles of the fish, as well as Bill, the man of my choice. Nobody told me I was to rear two babies with fish scales in their curls or that I would learn to change a diaper with one hand while keeping a steady tension on a spool reel with the other. I had to learn—or else.

Before our honeymoon was over, I was faced with a decision: I must become either a fishing-widow or a fishwife. If my husband chased salmon all over the Pacific Northwest without me, I would turn into a sad-eyed, introspective stay-at-home and, in time, resemble Whistler's Mother who I've always suspected was patiently waiting for some fisherman to come home. So with a prayer in my heart to my new patron saint, Izaac Walton, I chose to become a fishwife, my husband's companion on all his trips. This is a role not to be undertaken lightly, for it requires the touch of a lady, the heart of a lion, and the constitution of a jackass.

Many brides here in the state of Washington have to make up their minds just as I did, for this is the fisherman's Promised Land, overflowing with salmon, bass, trout—and more salmon. Seattle bankers and brokers read the tide charts in the morning paper before turning to the Wall Street listings, and they'll skip dinner when an incoming tide in the evening assures good fishing. It's half an hour from office to rowboat, as Seattle's business section is only a Paul Bunyan fly cast from Elliott Bay, our semi-landlocked harbor which is teeming with salmon.

In books fishermen are referred to as dreamy, vacant-eyed philosophers who spend more time assembling tackle than they do in stream or boat. But anglers don't dream around here. They fish. The line on one reel or another is damp the year round, except perhaps in early December. At that time, just before the opening of the steelhead season, a kindly Providence planned to have most salmon leave shallow water and stay at sea. It's pure luck that the absence of fish corresponds to the Christmas season when fishermen-family acquaintanceship is renewed and Father is pleased to see how much the children have grown since he last noticed them. This is the time to give Mother the split bamboo rod he himself has wanted so long, and in this land of abundance, hip boots instead of Christmas stockings are hung by the fireplace on Christmas Eve. Chrome and shiny brass spoons make dandy tree ornaments, and a spool of Monel metal line has it all over glass balls.

Of course not everybody out here fishes. There are a few sane and sober merchants, manufacturers, and grocers needed to cater to the fishermen. But at some time during any party or gathering, you'll see a cluster of men hanging on each other's words and there is sure to be a glitter in their eyes. Hands grip an imaginary rod, which suddenly jerks upward to show how that thirty-pounder snapped the leader and made off with all gear. Everybody offers advice and tells how the same thing *nearly* happened to him—and would have, except for that little trick he knows. The tall tales have started.

All fishermen are liars; it's an occupational disease with them like housemaid's knee or editor's ulcers. Deacons and doctors alike enlarge upon "the one that got away," measuring off with ecclesiastical or surgical fingers the size of the mythical monster. At this point, the uninitiated fishing-widow yawns, but the fishwife nods understandingly. Save face, save the ego at any price— too often it's all a fisherman brings home. I've heard sterling characters swear to the most unlikely stories simply to cover their humiliation. For it *is* embarrassing to have a wee bass outthink you. I've seen a fifteen-pound salmon make a sucker out of a top-flight executive and a

rainbow fool a psychology professor. Those big fish
don't get that way by being dumb; a trout that doesn't
think two jumps and several runs ahead of the average
fisherman is mighty apt to get fried. With light tackle,
fish get a fifty-fifty break and you don't need to pity
them. The term "poor fish" may be based upon their
uninteresting procreative habits, certainly not upon their
intelligence.

Before you go with us up the Skagit River for steelhead or to the San Juan Islands for king salmon, I want
to let you in on something. Did you know there's a roped-
off, high priority section of Heaven exclusively reserved
for the wives of fishermen? A celestial retreat unclut-
tered with leaky gas cans, rusty hooks, flooded motors,
kinked wire lines, and mangy fishing hats? Here there
will be no mention of incoming tides, three o'clock
breakfasts, too much or too little feed. The baked ambrosia will not have to be cleaned and scaled first. In
fact, the word "fish" never will be mentioned. This is
a well-earned reward for those who, on earth, nursed
husbands and sons through all the stages of fishing fever.

The symptoms? You know them well, no matter
which creek or coast you fish. There are those moments
of grandeur caused by a dozen twelve-inch trout, a mess
of silvers or a tremendous king salmon, a string of sea
bass or a couple of muskies. This is the time when Father
is insufferable, little heeding the words of his wife—or
Shakespeare, who reminds him that "Every braggart
shall be found an ass." Nearly bursting at the seams,
he phones all his cronies and they come on the run,
flocking around the dinner table like flies at a Sunday
School picnic. Father has his day; Mother, sagging
arches; and the cat has the milt.

But days of deepest depression surely will follow when none of the hundred-thousand-dollars' worth of plugs he owns (a fishwife's loose estimate) has any appeal, when frozen herring are so soggy they fall off the hook, or the fish just aren't there anyway. This can drag on for weeks. Sympathy, liver pills, or even benzedrine slipped into coffee does no good. Nothing helps this blue funk but a few pounds of fishy protoplasm on the business-end of a line. However, this treatment must be continued to keep run-of-the-millstream anglers happy during the legal season.

Watch out! Even when lakes or streams are closed by law, a careless whiff of clam chowder will send the inveterate fisherman off again. 'Way off. Then he gets that mellow, faraway look in his eye which changes to a fanatic gleam as he dashes to the basement. Gear comes rattling out of closets, reels are unwound, and the place becomes an obstacle course with yards of line criss-crossed all over it for inspection. Rusty spark plugs are scraped, oiled—and left to drip on the ironing board. Children are threatened with double hernia as they tug and strain, trying to help Father pull rods apart. The mingled smell of varnish and reel oil acts as a come-on, and feverishly new hooks are tied to hallowed plugs, toothmarked veterans of many battles. These are crooned over while wife and children are forgotten. There's the pungent odor of rubber cement as boots are patched and the sharp ammoniac tingle of brass polish. And you can count on it: there will be a worse stench when Father accidentally—but perennially—drops that half-used jar of spoiled bait eggs or the bottle of home-preserved herring. Both smell higher than an Indian village at sundown. At a time like this, if I mention a social engagement, Father is sure to develop a touch of lumbago, or any other dreamed-up ailment serious enough to keep him home—in the basement. He might as well be fishing!

Just like measles, this sort of thing is expected all over the country in early spring, but it is indigenous to the Puget Sound region where there is no closed season for salmon. At any ungodly moment, winter or summer, a fishwife must be booted and spurred and ready to go. I'm grateful that no fish bites best in total darkness. Now I like to fish, but I'm a convert; I wasn't born that way. However, unlike the addict, I can take it or leave it, and I'd rather leave it at four in the morning when a January gale is strong enough to blow salmon scales backward.

The Pacific Northwest climate is mild and the seasons sort of run together, but an experienced fisherman can tell the time of year by noting what kind of fish tails the cat is chewing on. Winter king salmon are rich, oily, and the best of the year, but they have the nastiest dispositions—not quite so mean, however, as the spring steelhead well downstream and thus still in the full flower of fish-hood. April trout hate to leave home, and summer's silver and king salmon seldom give a novice an even break. Fall brings the mighty hooknose silvers and cutthroat trout. You can see there's never a dull moment for fishermen out here.

Now I didn't know any of this—or suspect lots more —about a quarter of a century ago, when I was a girl and lived in Chicago. The state of Washington was just a half-inch pink square on the map and, like the rest of the Midwest and East, I thought Seattle had virgin forests

running between First and Second Avenues. I was
headed for a life on the prairie until I met Bill. He
changed my plans in a hurry. He breezed in from the
West with such a head of steam that I melted in my
tracks. He was attending a medical convention and,
after one disdainful look at the windy, dirty city, he began telling me about a glorious mountain world where
one could go hiking, skiing, or fishing and get home
again in time to make the gravy for the pot roast. He
told of shooting the rapids in an Indian canoe and about
his innumerable camping trips in the San Juan Islands.
He spoke of majestic Mt. Olympus and Mt. Constitution as though they were personal friends, and he promised me a trip through the ice caves of Mt. Rainier.

Of course he wedged in stories of fishing trips, so I
knew he was a fisherman, but I little guessed all that this
implied. He said I'd love it, too, and at the moment I
didn't give it a second thought. Bill was so nice and big
and brown, I would have been glad to go fishing for the
rest of my life on the River Styx. And so, innocently, I
rose to the fly and snapped at the lure.

He returned to Seattle. Mother and I followed him
west soon after. I little guessed how ill-prepared I was
for the life of a fishwife. I had been hand-raised by a
widowed mother, definitely a member of the old school
whose graduates have a Victorian hangover. To her,
fish have intestines, not guts; stomachs, not bellies; and
only female dogs are bitches. She thinks paper napkins
and horsey women abominations unto the Lord. Well-
bred and well-read, she taught me all the niceties of
living, which proved slightly inadequate for my role of
fishwife.

On the train, I reviewed all I knew about fishing.

Terrapin was a member of the social set and salmon always canned. Herring were shirtsleeve fish, caught already smoked or pickled. I thought cod must be easy to catch—any fish would welcome death whose liver smelled so vile. Trout came from streams and whitefish from traps.

I remembered certain gatherings where, with a dab of caviar-smeared toast in one hand and something iced in the other, I innocently had joined in the song which sympathizes with the poor virgin sturgeon which needs no urgin'. Roe was sautéed or canned. In those sheltered pre-fishing days, I would have shuddered to my shoes had I seen "caviar" taken on the hoof. Even today, as an old fishhand, it makes my stomach revolve to watch Indians grasp a ripe, squirming female and hold it a few inches above their upturned mouths. Then they bring the red, gooey eggs directly from producer to consumer, by using a stroking motion of thumb and forefinger along the underside of the belly. Much lip-smacking ensues while they grab another salmon and toss the old one to the squaws. Thanks. I'll take my caviar salted, pickled, spiced, dyed, and spread very thin.

The train rolled on through the wheat belt. Everything I owned was with me. My trousseau frothed with satin and lace numbers such as one sees advertised in *Vogue*: shimmering bed jackets and cobwebby lingerie. This was the age of pale pink ribbon and I had enough woven in and out of my undies to foul the rudder of a battleship. This was just standard equipment for a bride, I thought. Now I know that the Better Business Bureau should force advertisers to put footnotes on such pages, saying, "Above items of no possible use to a fisherman's bride." Wiser still, there should be a companion page featuring such lovelies as fishwives need: flannel pajamas, wool socks and shirts, blue jeans, hip boots, and long underwear (drop seat).

The prairies stretched out in such vast, endless miles that I had plenty of time for pre-marital jitters. Bill was a physician by profession, a sports fisherman by preference, and just how would this double-threat deal work out for me?

But all my fears were forgotten, magically erased from my mind when the train began to curl and twist through the Cascade Mountains of Washington. We had passed through the Rockies at night so the Cascades were the first mountains I'd ever seen—honest-to-God ones, ripped right out of *The National Geographic* and practically at my fingertips! The sky was a blue dome over a world of jagged peaks crowned with snow. Misty falls dropped hundreds of feet to the timberline. I was enchanted with the queer little trees that had such sturdy, thick trunks compared with their height. Each mountain fir, with its short, downswept branches to shed the snow, was a miracle of symmetry. Some of them grew right out of crevices in the rock, and I wondered if their struggle for existence gave them that sober chrome green so unlike the frivolous yellow-green of the alders in the valley below, where soil was deep and life was easy.

Now the train was threading its way along a shelf cut from a mountain side, and we were in a great bowl of sky-touching mountains. Everything was sharp and clear: the river that sparkled a thousand feet below us, the snow fields ten miles away, and the track that glinted like silver wires behind us. How did the train ever get up here? There didn't seem to be a single break in the wall of mountains, and I pondered over the vision and skill of those first engineers who had plotted this pass.

The train nosed on, searching its way through a labyrinth of peaks, each curve opening up new wonders. Those thin white threads against the jumble of rocks must be water falls hurtling down through distance and the ages. Near us was a rushing stream, cloudy with glacial silt. It boiled and tumbled down a mile-square façade of naked rock, and its spray nourished rock gardens on either side.

We passed over the Continental Divide and gradually the train lost altitude. Now we were in another world where everything was size forty-four. Only this time it was trees. I admitted to Mother that Bill's picture-postcards were not fakes—an automobile *could* drive through a tunneled-out fir. Where these giants thinned to just a scattering of hemlocks and spruce, there was a wild tangle of undergrowth. It was head high and I had a new respect for Lewis and Clark. Oregon is quite similar to Washington, and how could those intrepid explorers ever have cut through this to the coast?

Here a great fir had fallen, thundered to earth generations ago, and its flat, interlaced root structure stood up as tall as a one-story house. The trees dripped with yards of sage-green beard moss which added a sort of melancholy beauty. Everything—forests, mountains, vistas, trees, and sky—was scaled to majestic grandeur, and I wouldn't have been too amazed to see an armored dinosaur or mastodon peek around a cliff.

Regretfully, I said good-by to my mountains. Then, with little time to get set for such a surprise, we were coasting beside Puget Sound, running just a few feet above high-tide level. Entranced, I gazed over the shimmering Sound toward the Olympic Mountains. They were taller and more splendid than the Cascades—and mine to love forever.

Mountains are good for the ego—they cut one down to size. Man's strivings seem so finite in a land of these proportions; the Empire State Building would look puny backed up against even a minor-league mountain. I didn't realize it then, but at that moment I was beginning to become a Westerner.

The sea gulls flew beside us all the way into Seattle. The cars hitched to a stop, each little bump jerking me back to reality. The depot platform was grimy, gray, and depressing, but suddenly it became a lovely place. Bill was there.

2

All his worldly goods . . .

"Mother, Bill's terribly late. And for his own wedding!"

"Well, you asked for it, dear, when you promised to marry a doctor. It *is* twenty minutes of four, but he'll probably—" The words ran into a mumble as she adjusted my wedding dress.

"Bill said he was bringing my wedding present with him. Wonder what it is. Maybe I should take off these pearls, just in case. Should I?"

Mother didn't answer. She was peeking around the curtains of the bedroom window, watching guests come up the brick walk. Bill and I had rented a lovely colonial home in the Laurelhurst section of Seattle and were being married in it. Downstairs I could hear the restless murmur of voices, which conjured up visions of bride deserted at altar. Just then the telephone rang and I grabbed it from the bedside table.

"Darling," Bill said breathlessly, "I'm leaving the hospital right now. It was an emergency; didn't dream it would take this long. A ruptured appendix, most interesting case, and—"

"What interests me," I cut in, "is how long will it take you to get out here."

"I'll be there in fifteen minutes. Don't go ahead without me. 'By—and I love you."

"That's that," I said to Mother.

"No, my dear. That is just the beginning of that." It was three minutes of four when Bill burst into the room. Mother was horrified by such a breach of etiquette. Seeing the bride just before the service isn't done. But he did it, placating her with his charm and enthusiasm. He held me at arm's length, turned me around, admired my gray afternoon dress, and kissed me.

"Hope you didn't worry, honey. Darnedest appendix I ever saw. Now close your eyes. I left your wedding presents right outside the door." I did as he asked, wrinkling up my nose and asking, "Bill, will you always smell so strongly of ether?"

"Nope. 'Fraid not. Only after I'm lucky enough to operate. Now open your eyes."

He was standing there, radiant and mighty handsome with that well-scrubbed doctor look he has. If his brown eyes hadn't been so kind and his smile so winning, I never could have stood it, for he was holding out two hip-length rubber boots.

"Like 'em? They have non-skid soles but wait till

you see these!" He pulled a plaid wool shirt out of a bag and then a pair of blue jeans. Fortunately, I was too stunned to speak.

"That's not all!" He rushed back into the hall and returned with two long slender cloth cases that had some brown sticks with metal ends protruding from the open flaps.

"Split bamboo. *Female* bamboo. One for salmon, one for trout. I tried 'em for balance and they're perfect. And look at these." There were two spools with handles and gadgets on them, a big one and a pup. Then he proudly handed me an oblong metal box, saying, "It's all fitted out. Rust-proof, too." He looked at me expectantly. "Like 'em?"

It was just as well I didn't have time to answer. Bill's sister was standing in the doorway, beckoning him urgently. Still beaming, he kissed me and tore out of the room. After he had left, I looked at Mother—a long, long look.

When the ceremony was over, there was a blur of kisses and best wishes. I suppose I nibbled at a petit-four and I hope I gave appropriate replies to Bill's friends. None of mine were there, and a lonesome feeling it is not to recognize a single guest at your own wedding. I was glad to change into a white linen suit and dash to the car with him. As we shot out of the driveway in his Buick roadster, rice bounced off the fenders like hail.

"Where we going? Can't you tell the bride by now? Remember, you promised we wouldn't fish on our honeymoon."

"Of course not, darling. I wouldn't think of it. We're

going to Orcas Island and stay at a most lady-like inn. You'll love it."

I wasn't so sure, but I was thrilled by the beautiful countryside we drove through. Soon we were on the highway that skirts the Sound and I relaxed completely when I saw the Olympic Mountains as we hummed through the LaConnor flats. Under the spell of their benevolence, little nagging fears slipped away and I warmed to Bill's nearness and dearness. We drove about ninety miles to the cunning little town of Anacortes where the ferry was waiting at the slip. It looked like a great white mother duck ready to welcome us under her wings. After we were aboard, he leaned forward to lock the ignition. A white tissue-paper package poked out of his coat pocket.

"What's that?"

"Oh! I forgot. Another present for you, dear." I opened the small rectangular box slowly, half expecting to find a platinum-plated herring or, at best, one of those spoons he was always talking about. Then I lifted the lid and there was the loveliest little watch I'd ever seen. I gazed at it for a long time and slowly it pulled out of shape, for I was seeing it through tears.

"Hey! What you doing? Good Lord, it's only a watch. What's the matter?" He put his arm around me and gave me his handkerchief. I dried my eyes and smiled. There was no use explaining that it was lots more than a watch to me.

We stood on the top deck of the ferry and watched the sun slip down behind the San Juan Islands, an archipelago of more than one hundred islands. Almost all of them are heavily timbered with cedar, fir, spruce, or hemlock and some of them looked like rounded green gumdrops as they nestled down in this beautiful inland sea. Bill pointed behind us toward the Cascade range asking, "Do you like your mountains served up white, bronze, or purple? But don't bother to choose. As soon as the sun really sets, you'll have all three colors, one right after the other. Now, for my taste, I like purple best, 'cause that's when the king salmon hit."

The waddling ferry picked its way through a maze of islands, across Rosario Strait, and through narrow Thatcher's Pass. Some of the islands were small; others were several miles in length and had rugged, rocky shores. It was a brand-new world to me and one of breathtaking beauty.

"Look! Down there." Bill pointed to the sleek black head of a seal as it bobbed up not far from the boat. It submerged and then popped up again. Near it, jaunty black birds with scarlet feet seemed intent upon committing suicide, diving below the surface as the boat approached, and staying down.

"They're called 'Helldivers,' " Bill said, "sort of a country cousin of a duck." Gulls screamed and darted after food thrown in the ship's wake, fighting loudly over bits of it. A large, ripe moon swam into view, completing the stage set.

"Good moon," Bill said.

"Aren't all moons good?"

"Not on your life. The waning crescent moon is terrible."

"Oh, darling," I purred, "you're just in love. You don't know what you're talking about."

"I certainly do. The full moon brings the biggest dips in the tide, the very high and the extreme minus tides.

Now, salmon generally come in when the low slack-tide begins to flood. You see, the herring—"

"Bill!" I cut him short. "Are there fish scales on everything you see? You should have married a mermaid." He pursed his lips in thought, ran thumb and fingers along his jaw while giving the matter heavy consideration.

"No. You'll do, till one comes along. See those lights ahead? That's Orcas." And a short time later we nudged the ferry slip, our speed cut by starting the propellers in reverse, and deep blue water was churned into green with curling white edges. With hardly a jar, the ferry brushed against the pilings and was made fast.

The drive to the inn was exciting, not that I could see anything in the darkness, but there were wonderful new smells: the sharp ping of cedar and tang of ripe apples in the orchards; the mossy, earthy sweetness of woods and the blood-tingling sharpness of salt air. My faith in my husband reached an all-time high when I saw the inn, a low, rambling, modernized farmhouse. Moonlight filtered through madrona trees, etching black lace patterns on the lawn. My happiness was complete—this was no tar-paper fishing joint.

The next morning we had breakfast beside a window that looked down the length of East Sound. The waves sparkled and threw off splinters of light; great puffy clouds, blown up to the bursting point, hung motionless over the water. There was color everywhere: green grass and trees, indigo water, and brown rocks in soft, half-tone shades. Bill explained how sunshine, coming through salt-laden mist, is filtered; it is warm but not harshly glaring. A shielding screen of haze, stretched above the clouds from three mountain ranges, decreed that this be a gentle land.

"Now," Bill said, finishing his third cup of coffee, "what will we do today? There's a low tide this morning. We could dig little clams, medium-sized clams, or horse clams. Umm. Incoming tide until noon." After a dreamy silence which practically smelled of fish, he forced himself to continue. "We could drive up Mount Constitution or go horseback riding. Or rowing. Say," he perked up at once, "maybe you'd like to meet Cappy Bell?"

"Is he a fisherman?" I was suspicious and on guard.

"Ye-es," he admitted, "but the swellest old codger you ever saw. A herring fisherman and—"

"He can wait," I said firmly. "I wouldn't trust you around a fisherman, especially since I saw all that gear in the trunk of the car. You brought my wedding presents, too. How come?"

He didn't answer and we left the dining room and wandered over the sand flats of Crescent Beach.

Hours later, when the tide was high, I still was loath to leave this marine wonderland of sand dabs, moon snails, hermit crabs, and spouting clams. Reluctantly, I got in the car and we started up Mount Constitution. We drove through Moran State Park, with its Columbus-old fir trees, and skirted Cascade Lake, which dimpled and danced like a great bowl of quicksilver.

"Rainbows," Bill said, nodding in the general direction of the lake.

"Where?" I asked, puzzled. Instinctively I looked up into the sunlit sky. Bill smiled and shook his head sadly, implying that I had a lot to learn about a country where one looked *down* for rainbows, not up.

Now we were winding up the steep road which led to the summit of Mount Constitution. Trees on either side of us dripped with sage-green beard moss, yard-long wisps of fluffy stuff. There were miles of Christmas trees already trimmed. When we could drive no farther, we parked the car and walked up the little knoll ahead of us. When I first looked about I couldn't find a word to say. I just stood there on the top of this mountain world, transfixed. For there at our feet, stretched out as far as the eye could see in every direction, was a universe of sea and mountains and islands. There were dozens of islands, like irregularly shaped emeralds set in a blue network of channels.

"Bill," I said slowly, hardly breathing, "I just don't believe it."

"You *should* like it. Travelers say it's the second best marine view in the United States. The scene from Diamond Head in Hawaii rates first." We gazed down— two thousand five hundred feet down—to the royal blue water in the deep channels where boats were impossible little matchsticks.

"Kind of like sitting on a cloud and watching the world beneath you, isn't it?" And Bill began naming the different islands as though they were old friends: Sucia, Cypress, Blakely, Lummi, Clark, and Barnes. He pointed out others and told me something about each one.

"See Twin Lakes below us, halfway up the mountain?" The two round little lakes, nearly touching each other, appeared, from where we stood so far above them, to be chiseled out of treetops. Set in a thicket of well-brushed evergreens, they glowed warmly, like something alive. He told me there was a wonderful

name for such lakes in the German language. "It's
Gottesaugen, which means 'God's eyes.'" He pointed
a bit to the right and said that the other lake was called
Mountain Lake. He started to rave about the trout,
said that at sundown he often had his limit in an hour
or so. When he began measuring them off with his
fingers, I stopped him, treating him like a reformed
drunkard, afraid one little sip would make him forget
his promise.

Time slipped past and now Mount Baker, reflecting
the rose of sunset, seemed blanketed in strawberry ice
cream, and three chains of mountains were floating in
a powder blue mist.

As we drove down the mountainside, I told Bill, "I'm
coming back here. Again and again and again. There
couldn't be a dream more wonderful than this."

"Sometime," he said, "we'll camp out all night up here.
Put our sleeping bags on a bed of moss. All four of 'em."

"Four?"

"Sure. Bill junior—and maybe a Bob? We'll have a
Cook's Tour over every nook and bay in the San Juan
Islands. Like the idea?"

One afternoon near the end of our stay on the island
we were sitting in the country store in East Sound. We
were perched on stools eating chocolate sundaes and
doting on the orderly confusion of Templin's General
Emporium where cosmetics and the veterinary's "Bag
Balm" are kept on the same shelf. Suddenly Bill jumped
up and tore over to an old man who had just entered.

"Cappy Bell! You old herring hound." Bill thumped
him on the back and pumped his hand. "Am I glad to
see you! Where you been?"

"Fishin'," Cappy drawled. He took off his duckbill cap and scratched his bristly white hair with his thumb. So this was Bill's fishing pal; I looked him over well. He was of medium height but he appeared short, for his shoulders were loosened and stooped with age. He had dangling, long arms and his knees jutted forward when he walked, reminding me of a puppet whose strings were manipulated by an inexperienced hand. His faded blue overalls and matching coat hung limp and floppy, and his sagging hip boots were spangled with fish scales. There was a similar sequined effect running up and down his thighs where he must have rubbed his hands.

"Where you been, Bill? Missed you. Don'cha know the silvers are goin' crazy at Waldron Island?" The way he cocked his head on one side and something about his sharp-pointed nose and bright eyes made me think of a robin when it first spots a worm. Cappy rubbed a gnarled hand over his face, its skin resembling a side of dried codfish. Bill had told me he was a herring fisherman, and I identified him with the only herring I'd ever seen which were salty, spicy, and pungent.

"Say, Bill," he said, fondly poking him in the ribs, "glad yuh got the sense to quit peddling pills when there's a good run on. How about takin' a crack at 'em tomorrow?"

"Sure thing, Cappy. And I want you to meet my—"

"Ain't got time for no more sociability. Tide's turnin'. Come on over 'bout ten." He tossed a coin in the general direction of a clerk, chose a plug of chewing tobacco, nodded at Bill and left the store.

The next day as we drove to Point Lawrence to meet Cappy Bell, I kept a tight leash on my martyr complex, figuring Bill honestly rated one day of fishing. It wasn't hard, for the sun had burned off the pre-September mist and the day was gloriously golden and warm. I was wearing my "wedding present" clothes and I liked my first red plaid shirt. But the jeans were not so good, fitting a trifle too quickly here and there, mostly there. The boots were hot and didn't do a thing for me.

"Bill," I said, "I'll never be voted 'Miss San Juan' in this getup."

"Don't you care," he comforted. "You'd win hands down except for one thing: the fish around here can't vote because most of them are Canadians by birth. They're just stalling around for a while before heading up the Frazier River on the Canadian boundary line. They're foreigners."

"Bill, tell me about Cappy Bell."

"Well, he's a great old guy, a stubborn cuss, but a mighty good friend. Side by side, he could outfish an Indian. He used to be a freight boat and a tugboat captain. Now he lives at Point Lawrence during the summer and keeps his live bait box full of herring. Sells 'em to the sports fishermen and makes a living at it, too. That's his work. When he plays, he goes fishing for salmon. It's quite a sight to see Cappy net herring, especially when he uses a fine-mesh, long-handled net. He just scoops the small ones up. Gigs for big herring."

"Gigs? What-do-you-mean?" I wasn't following this.

"Oh," Bill chuckled, "it's a way of catching herring with a line and shiny hooks. I'll explain it later. Now, generally, there's nothing that swims or floats smart enough to fool Cappy, but he tells of one time when he was slapped back on his haunches. He was out for three-

inch herring and he was rowing, off Kangaroo Point.
The tide was boiling, bringing in so many herring that
Cappy figured he could land some with his huge hand
net. Just ahead of him he heard the gulls go crazy, and
he looked around to see dozens of them shrieking and
diving at a small area which was a-shine with floating
fish scales. So he leaned on his oars and hightailed it to
the herring ball."

"The what?" I interrupted.

"A herring ball," Bill expounded patiently, "is just
what it sounds like: a big ball of herring, sometimes several feet in diameter. You see, when Helldivers, those
black birds that look like underprivileged ducks, dive
under a school of small herring and the gulls start working them over from above, the herring pack themselves
into a tight ball for protection. They knock off a lot
of scales in the rumpus, which attracts the sea gulls.

"Well, as I was saying, Cappy had rowed to the spot
and, sure enough, just a couple of feet under the surface
was a dark, silver-flecked ball of fish. He grabbed his
net, stood up in the boat, and was all ready to swipe
down under that ball when a great dark shape slid right
up beside the boat. No more herring. Old Satchel
Mouth—he's the whale that hangs around here—had
scooped up the whole ball right under Cappy's nose.
When he told me about it two days later, he was still
swearing—and when Cappy really lets go, it's enough
to turn the tide back. He said that whale cost him a
month's supply of gin, but I kind of doubt that. I don't
believe there ever was a herring ball that big. Anyway,
the yarn's true. Cappy's okay."

I wasn't so sure, and I wondered about him as we
turned down a road that descended sharply to Point

Lawrence. On the mainland in the blue distance were the Cascade Mountains with Mount Baker lording it over all creation. Lummi, Cypress, and the Peapod Rocks circled the horizon, and the water off the Point was churning and tide-torn. We parked the car behind the boathouse, near the cabins that were scattered about, and walked down to the curved, pebbly beach.

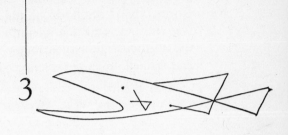

"*I ain't takin' no women*"

"Cabin" was an elegant name for Cappy's tar-paper lean-to sagging between two poles. The roof was made of flattened-out oil cans. It had two smudged windows, and from the door which hung drunkenly on a single hinge, trash overflowed in all directions. A dejected-looking outboard motor was clamped on a barrel of oily water and near by were sundry wash tubs, fish poles, buckets, old boots, tin cans, and a noteworthy collection of gin bottles. Leaning against the house was a bundle of splintered oars draped with fish nets. The whole picture, including Cappy himself wasn't very reassuring, but then, a man called "Cappy" certainly must have a boat, which I imagined

to be one of those sturdy little high-busted jobs I had
seen on the Sound. A day on the water would be fine.
The men could fish all they pleased; I'd fluff up some
pillows and bask in the sunshine.

"Hi," Cappy called to Bill with a yard-wide smile.
Then he saw me and his Santa Claus eyebrows pulled
together in a frown. "Who's that?"

"Oh, I tried to tell you yesterday," Bill answered.
"This is Bea, my wife. We were married last week."

"You ain't figgerin' on takin' her along?" He ran his
tongue around his cheeks and spat pure venom.

"Sure I am. She's got to learn to fish sometime and
she couldn't have a better teacher."

"Well, I ain't takin' her. Never been a petticoat
across the gun'l yit and I ain't startin' now, by God."

"Now, Cappy, you two are going to like each other.
She won't get in the way."

" 'Tain't that."

"But it's our honeymoon. I can't leave her."

"I'm not goin' to have her aboard. Got my reasons."

"Listen, Cappy," Bill said, getting a little edgy, "all
the years we've been fishing together we've never had
an argument. You're not going to let me down now,
are you?"

"Nope. Not you. But I still ain't takin' no women
on a fishing trip."

"Why not?" Bill demanded angrily.

"Oh, Doc, don't be so god almighty dumb. Lean
down and I'll tell yuh."

While he whispered in Bill's ear, I got madder and
madder, but I wasn't going to let that stinging in my
eyes get out of control. The contrary old cuss! What
did Bill see in him anyway?

Then I heard Bill laugh, but he sobered immediately and thoughtfully stroked his jaw. After a moment his eyes lit up and he snapped his fingers, saying, "I've got it, Cappy. It'll be okay." Grinning, he walked off to the boathouse and returned with a huge beach umbrella.

"Now you can take her. I'll give her a high-sign, you can hide behind the umbrella, and there we are, all set. Simple as horsing in a trout on a wire line." Cappy didn't answer, but he glared at me and grunted something about women on a fishing trip being as unnecessary as teats on a snake. He stalked off to the water's edge.

I was furious and just as I decided to jump in the car, drive back to the inn, and let Bill figure out how to get home, I caught sight of the only boat in the bay, a sweet little cruiser riding at anchor. It must be Cappy's and a trip on that would be something. I wouldn't speak to the men. They could fish or turn somersaults for all I cared. I sat down on a log to wait.

Bill was rowing the old man out toward the cruiser, but suddenly they stopped short of it and Cappy Bell leapt aboard something that looked like a floating platform with a rim on it. I hadn't even noticed it before. Now Cappy was standing up and skulling the clumsy hulk in; it was unpainted, blunt-nosed at both ends, and almost unmanageable. When it still was quite a way off shore, I got the first nauseous whiff on an incoming breeze. Fish! Rotten fish. Ten million herring must have bled and died aboard. Compared to sun-ripened fish, the Chicago stockyards back home were like roses in the morning dew. Unnerved, I just gaped at the punt —and pinched my nose.

However, Bill didn't appear to notice anything. Arms

loaded, he was wading out to the tops of his boots, stowing gear in this baby barge while Cappy held it off shore with an oar. The big beach umbrella Cappy kicked under a seat, but he was more careful with the rods and tackle boxes. Bill actually was singing as he heaved his own outboard motor aboard. He motioned me to wade out while he swung a big galvanized wash tub over the side. A wash tub on a fishing trip? I thought he'd lost his mind.

Gingerly I sat down on one of the encrusted seats and watched Cappy tinker with the one-lung, inboard motor. He cranked it but it wheezed and died. This happened half a dozen times and I was perversely glad that it was as mean-tempered as he was. Another crank, and the tubercular motor coughed violently, sputtered—and died. The blue smoke could have come from the exhaust or the words Cappy directed at it. He cranked again, cursing softly, richly, and roundly. Bill offered to help, but the old man shoved him away, saying, "This hellcat's got a kick worse'n corn whisky. It might bust your high-priced operatin' arm. Don't matter 'bout me—I'm ready to fall apart anyhow." He straightened up and fumbled under some foul-looking blankets, saying, "Guess I'm priming the wrong engine." With that he picked up a bottle of gin, twisted the cork out, and tipped his head back, pouring about a fourth of a pint down at one gulp. Then he shook his head, blinked, and emitted a long-drawn-out breath that could have been ignited.

"Ought to go now," he grinned. And it did, for the flywheel spun on the very next crank. While Cappy had been fussing around, Bill had poled out to the bait box and had dipped several dozen large, squirming her-

ring into the wash tub that was half filled with water.
Sorry as I was for the frantic fish, I was relieved to know
there was a reason for the tub.

We headed around the point and soon were skirting
a high rock bluff where moss and crisp little ferns grew
in the crevices. The men, side by side on the rear seat,
were chatting happily, their words lost to me by the
intermittent chug of the motor. I felt sure Bill gladly
would furnish bail if Cappy committed forty-four kinds
of mayhem and broke all ten commandments at one fell
swoop. These friends were like two circles that touched
only at a single point, but a binding point—fishing.

Even going with the tide, our lumbering craft was
making so little speed that Bill put his outboard motor
on the rack made for a motor and fast to the stern. With
both propellers behind us, our punt was thrust ahead
faster. But Cappy grumbled good-naturedly at Bill,
shouting, "That's the trouble with you folks today. Always hurrin' so you git your tail in a knot."

He handed the tiller to Bill and used a lard pail to dip
half the water out of the tub of herring. He replaced
it with fresh sea water which did seem to perk up the
fish considerably. I admired them as they raced around
in circles, but if I ever had seen a rainbow trout with
its delicate, multicolored scales, I wouldn't have wasted
any adjectives on herring. For they have nasty expres-
sions and coarse scales of silver, with only a little blatant
purple on their backs. But at the moment, I felt a kin-
ship for them: we both were trapped in this evil-smelling
craft.

We had left Point Doughty on the coast of Orcas and
now were halfway across President's Channel which runs
between Orcas and Waldron Islands. I was facing for-

ward and sitting in the bow, or what would have been
the bow in a respectable boat, and ignoring the men.
The high sandy banks of Point Hammond on Waldron
Island were close now. Bill called to me, "Bea, keep
your eyes peeled for kelp. And say," he added, "don't
look now, but there's a mountain watching us."

I squirmed around on the scaly seat and looked over
my shoulder. There, behind me, practically in my hip
pocket, was lovely symmetrical Mount Baker iced with
clouds. Its reflection in the water was a ten-mile-long
white cone that rippled with each wave.

Bill and Cappy, each hugging a tiller under his arm,
were setting up gear. Tackle boxes were open and stuff
spread all over. Bill's sleek, shiny rod was quite a contrast to Cappy's pole, which was unvarnished yellow
bamboo with permanent curvature of the spine. The old
man eyed Bill's reel, spit well over the side, and said,
"See you're using that new-fangled wire line. 'Tain't
worth the trouble. Gits more kinks in it than an old-
age pensioner. Give me cuddyhunk."

"You can have it, Cappy. Who wants to play a salmon
with half a pound of lead on his nose? Wire line gets
you down deep with just a couple of ounces. And say,
I'll buy you a bottle of gin if this number four, half-and-
half McMahon spoon won't land 'em today. I'm feeling
lucky."

"You'll have to be—to git 'em on that rig. Only a
damn fool would offer salmon tin when they want
herring. They're still feeding around here, you know."
With that, he plunged his hand into the tub of herring,
picked out an actively swimming one, and stuck the lead
hook on the setup through its jaw while it was still alive.
Shuddering, I faced forward, and just in time, too, for

ahead I saw a great snake's nest, slithering brown things coiling all over each other in the water.

"Bill! What's that?" He jumped up, looked, and grabbed both tillers, swinging them hard, which jerked the ambling craft to one side. We missed the stuff by inches, but the sudden jolt sent half the water sloshing out of the herring tub where it trickled all over the deck. It soaked the big beach umbrella, almost got the lunch boxes, tipped over a can of metal polish, but worst of all, this drenching brought forth any dormant flavor left in the boat. A new and fearsome stench arose.

"Thanks for spotting the kelp, Bea—but you might do it sooner next time. If you don't, I'll revoke your first mate's papers. How about you pouring some more water on the herring? We're busy now. Here's the pail." I kneeled down, put the bucket in wrong, open-end forward, and it was nearly snatched out of my hands. But I finally managed to heave a lot of water into the tub. Some of it splashed out, adding new rivulets to the mess already underfoot. So I pulled out a rag from under a seat and started to mop up the place, expecting a kind word for this housewifely action. But Cappy glanced at me and yelled, "Quit it. You got my polishin' rag." Even he must have noticed the added aroma for he said, "A good rich smell like this helps preserve the deck. Keeps the weather out. Herrin' oil's as penetratin' as linseed, an' cheaper. Let it be." And so I did, right where I'd flung it, and went back to my seat.

Bill laid aside the rod he had set up and took another from its case. My wedding present! He grinned at me, saying, "Didn't know when I brought it along that we'd be using this. Lesson number one. Better come see how I rig it up." In a nice soothing voice reserved for idiots and wives, he explained everything as he went along.

"Now the first thing to do in putting a rod together is to rub the butt end of the ferule on your nose and—"

"Wouldn't a rabbit's foot be better?" This time I was sure he was kidding.

" 'Course not. The oil from your skin lubricates the two parts of the rod enough to make them pull apart more easily." He glanced around and said we were near enough to the fishing grounds to stop the outboard motor, which he did, tilting it up on the rack out of the way. While Bill screwed on my reel and threaded the line through the guides, I watched Cappy put his herring *still alive* on his triple-hook setup. He fussed with those triple hooks for a long time, jabbing one prong of each in either side of the herring. The single steelhead hook, about five inches above the bottom triple hook, came up through the herring's jaw. Bill called this an "Orcas Island setup" and said it was good for both kings and silvers but had to be adjusted differently for each of them. Kings like a slowly revolving roll while silvers strike a faster, fluttering bait. Finally Cappy eased the leader with wriggling herring over the side, set the eight-ounce slip sinker back about fifteen feet, and peered down at the herring, critically inspecting its action.

"Looks good, Cappy," Bill said. "That's a swell shimmy you have on it. A touch of the master."

"Yep, it's okay. That herring's own mother would never guess he's in trouble. When you git a lick of sense, you'll heave that hardware out and use live bait, too. Say, I clean forgot to give it my blessing." With that he reeled in, carefully lifted the fluttering herring out of the water, and spit on it. "No use temptin' fate." Dead-pan, he let the line out again and stripped out fifty feet. Then he settled back to enjoy life.

Bill explained how a star drag reel works, how slack line can be prevented because one may reel in even when line is being pulled out. The second the run stops, line comes in.

"This is forty-pound test cuddyhunk." Bill nudged Cappy and added, "For beginners." Cappy Bell just recrossed his legs and spit.

"Now I'm putting on a six-ounce slip sinker. Here at the end of the line I'm attaching a one-ounce crescent sinker, tying it into the swivel ring. This is called piano wire leader. Number three is about right for these babies and I'm cutting a six-foot length, see?"

One end of the leader he attached to the ring in the swivel and on the other end he twisted on a beautiful little mother-of-pearl gadget. "This is called a 'Pearl Wobbler' and it has more lure than a fan dancer. And even more wiggles. It gets 'em." He stood up and started to toss my rig over the side, but I grabbed it back and spit on it.

"Learnin'," Cappy nodded approvingly. "Don't pay to take no chances." Bill showed me how to pull out some eighty feet of line and then said, "Sit up forward and face us and keep that rod out straight to one side."

Cappy fished on the other side of the boat while Bill let his line fall back over the back of the boat. He seemed to judge the trolling speed of the boat and decide it was all right, so he sat down and relaxed. He slapped Cappy affectionately on one knee. Both men were wearing those beatific smiles which reminded me of a couple of he-Mona Lisas.

I looked around at the islands which had seemed to be such tiny dabs of land when I had looked down on them from Mount Constitution. But now, on a level with them, I could see the little coves which indented their shores, I knew their names, and they seemed like old friends. Herring gulls, much like sea gulls only smaller, dotted the water, and elongated sooty black birds flew over us. Their necks looked like six inches of garden hose. Bill called them loons or shags. Near by, hundreds and hundreds of sea gulls wheeled over a tiny island not more than two city blocks in circumference. It was enchanting to watch them tilt and dip into the air currents or take breakneck dives toward the shiny golden grass that covered the top of the rocky island. Their incessant and mournful cries tore at my nerves, but they were a beautiful sight. Highlighted by the sun, they looked like a mighty handful of silver and white confetti fluttering down from the sky.

"That's the sea gull's Niagara Falls," Bill said. "They come here from miles around during the nesting season. We'll call on them some spring when the eggs are hatching and you may cuddle a baby gull in your hands—if you can catch him. They are cute little balls of black-spotted down but they're sure full of hell-fire."

"You hadn't better," Cappy drawled, "unless you like the stripes on your suit going around instead of up and down. That's a bird sanctuary. Protected by law." He pointed to a larger island near us and said that it was called Skipjeck. "It's lousy with rabbits but I never could figure it out. There's no water on the island—guess they must drink beer. Which reminds me of somethin' I pretty near forgot."

"Tell me," I cut in hastily, in hopes he wouldn't drag

out the gin again, "how will I know if I get a fish on? What'll I do?"

"You don't do nothin' but hang onto the pole," Cappy replied laconically. "The salmon does the rest."

Bill tapped his rod and, in a stage whisper, said, "It's called a rod, not a pole."

Cappy Bell grunted. "Them city-slicker rigs of yours are rods; mine's a pole. Anything over a dollar ninety-eight is a rod. Looks good but it don't catch any more fish." He looked down at the water rippling beside the boat and said to Bill, "Better give the engine a little more juice. We're not goin' quite fast enough for silvers in this here current."

We were trolling some three hundred feet off shore in Severson's Bay on the sunset side of Waldron Island. Bill told me to shorten my line or I'd get bottom, and every few minutes I had to haul it all in to clean off the eel grass.

"Salmon ain't jumpin'. That's a good sign," Cappy commented.

"That sounds silly," I said. "I should think you'd be glad to know if they are here."

"They're here. No doubt about that. The way the herrin' is boilin', somethin' is stirrin' 'em up. 'Tain't blackfish. Now, about salmon jumpin'. They generally do it for one of three reasons and none of them good for the fisherman. Either they are trying to shake off sea lice which cling around their—"

"Vents," Bill broke in quickly.

"Okay, their vents." Cappy winked at him and continued, "Or they're bein' chased by porpoise or seals. Or mebbe they're just playin'. Anyhow they ain't thinkin' about food."

When Cappy Bell wasn't snapping my head off, his sly humor and infinite lore were amusing. I wondered how he could drink so much and never show it, but he seemed as sober as a judge ought to be.

There was still no sign of fish and the men began to fret. Ours was the only boat on the water and there was not a sign of habitation anywhere despite the two dozen families that Cappy said lived on the island. Just sea, mountains, and islands. And a hundred million acres of blue sky. Driftwood, bleached by sun and salt to a silvery gray, was piled into grotesque patterns on the beach. Tremendous logs, all of four feet through, lay above the high-tide mark, silent testimony of the fury of the winter gales. Great chunks of trees, roots and all, had been wedged into crevices between the rocks on those jutting promontories. Evidently, this smiling land was not always so gentle as it seemed.

Suddenly Cappy leaned over to Bill and spoke in his ear. My husband flashed me a wicked grin, secured the handle of his fishing rod between the bait tub and a tackle box, and said, "Now don't ask questions, Bea. Just turn around and face straight ahead. Don't turn back till I whistle." I caught a glimpse of him grabbing the beach umbrella as I obediently swung about on the seat, and I fleetingly wondered what new mumbo jumbo this was and how it fitted into the rest of their heathen rites, while I gazed contentedly across the international boundary line toward the soaring Selkirk Mountains.

Then it happened! I jumped up, yelling and scared. "Hey, Bill! I'm losing all my string." The line started jerking as it ripped off the reel and, as I was pulled around, my line smacked into the raised umbrella which hid both men. With a clatter and to the tune of some

sea-going oaths, the umbrella tumbled back into the
boat just as a coffee can was tossed overboard. Shame-
faced, Cappy was fumbling with buttons. Bill picked up
his rod, reeled in, and said something about Cappy being
a charter member of The Overside Yacht Club. He
was trying hard not to laugh. A minute later the old
man killed the engine when he meant to throw it into
neutral, picked up his pole and glowered at me, saying,
"Time and tide ain't the only things that don't wait."
Savagely, he added, "What in hell you hollerin' for?
You just got a fish on."

"What'll I do?" I squeaked as more line pulled out.

"Let him go. He ain't goin' no place." I thought both
men were indifferent to my plight for they were calmly
bringing in their own lines.

"You men make me sick. One of you could help me.
Why should I let this fish run any more? He's had years
to run all he wants to. Now I want him to come in!"
Just then Bill flipped his leader into the boat and jumped
to my side.

"Easy does it. Keep the tip of your rod up; let him
pull against the spring of it. Now start reeling in . . ."

"Why?" I exploded. "It's still going out."

"That's what the drag reel is for—keeps a steady tension on him. Don't let him have any slack or he'll throw
the hook. Careful, reel in faster." Now the line had
stopped its outward rush and came in easily. This was
simple—no pull at all. I was bringing in a fish. Feeling
sure I was about to land my antagonist, I spoke jauntily
to Cappy, "Better get the net. I'll be needing it soon."
I'd show him I could handle this situation once I had
the knack of it. Nothing to it. But Cappy Bell lazily
reached into his pocket for a jackknife and then under

the seat for a bit of driftwood and began to whittle, drawling, "Hell, I got half an hour yet."

Just then pandemonium broke loose about ten feet from the boat. Something green and silver corkscrewed out of the water, spiraled into the air, and fell back with a resounding splash. Now, as though a madman had hold of the line, it ripped off that humming reel. The faster it went, the harder I yelled.

"Still in a hurry?" Cappy taunted, his head cocked on one side and his blue eyes squinting in amusement. "That salmon don't want to be baked. None of 'em do."

Again I reeled the fish in, matching my will against his. When my arms were ready to fall apart at the joints, Bill warned me, "Get set. He'll probably take another run when he sees the boat." But suddenly the line went limp.

"He's gone, Bill!"

"Not necessarily. He's just coming in faster than you are reeling. Keep winding—and keep cool." Fine advice! Bill was as excited as I was and just itching to take my rod. If I'd been stone deaf in Siberia, I could have heard him shout at me: "Reel faster. Get that slack line in!"

Soon the slip sinker bumped into the tip of the rod and slid down the line. I was worried, afraid something had broken, but forgot it when Bill pointed down to the water. There was my salmon. I looked closer, half hoping, half scared to see the thing. It was almost two feet long and as it rolled drunkenly in the water, I caught a glimpse of silver sides below the greenish back.

Then there was an explosion. That salmon reared up on its tail and shook its head violently from side to side. He kicked up buckets of water before he dived under the boat. The rod bent in a sharp curve, the tip well under the boat, and the line raced out.

"Go to the stern! Follow him around," Bill yelled. When I just stood there and looked at him blankly without moving, he shoved me and snapped, "That's the back of the boat, dummy. Work the rod around and remember the propeller. Lose that fish and I'll divorce you." I managed to do as he told me and the line went zinging out, cutting a widening V where it entered the water. Bill showed me how to "pump" him in this time by letting the tip of the rod down almost horizontal and then raising it slowly and steadily, using the spring of the rod to put extra pull on the line.

"Balky as a she-mule, ain't it?" Cappy said contentedly without looking up from his whittling. "Must be a female. Males ain't so cussed. Ever."

The line inched back on the reel. Between chills and fever of excitement, I was winding my own fast-diminishing strength on that spool. My backbone was unraveling and I knew my fingers never would uncurl.

"There he is!" Bill pointed down beside the boat. "And d-a-r-l-i-n-g, if you don't want me sent up for wife beating, keep the tip of your rod up. That's it. Now lead him into the net." He told me to keep calm but his own voice was skidding over several octaves.

"No, watch. See what you're doing? Get his head up out of the water so I can come up under him." The net whisked through the water, scooped up the battling salmon, and Bill swung it into the boat. While the silver salmon thrashed and pounded in the net, Bill let go of the long handle and threw his arms around me, giving me lung-loosening thumps on my back. I sagged in his arms.

"Gosh," I breathed, "it's big. And isn't it beautiful?"

Cappy snorted, "Quit your necking. Let's go after his brothers and sisters; they're just as handsome. Hand me my pole."

"That's a hell of a good silver," Bill was musing. "It'll go seven, eight pounds. Maybe more. Get that lead pipe and I'll show you how to settle an argument."

I was scared silly of the thing as it twisted about in the mesh of the net, but Bill made me grasp it firmly on its slimy, ice-cold back. Then he took over and rapped it sharply on the back of its head. It shuddered convulsively for a moment and then flattened down, inert. Perhaps it was fatigue or the sight of something being killed that made me shaky all over. I was ready to lie down beside my fish and match him quiver for quiver. My heart was still kicking me in the ribs.

"Bill," I sighed, "I've never been so excited and mad and glad all at once in my life. Never."

"That's fishing," he said cheerily as he took the pliers and extracted the hook on the pearl wobbler from the salmon's mouth. I was admiring the iridescent sheen of the silver scales and its smooth, streamlined beauty. It had such a nice figure—no alderman's stomach like pictures I'd seen of fresh-water fish. Its sharp-toothed, belligerent jaws were chiseled out of gun metal. The deeply notched tail was a good four inches across, fluting out from a wrist that was compact and strong. I had felt the force of its strike and its speed in the water. Now I could see how well-equipped salmon were to fight off the countless hazards of the sea.

Bill had pushed it into the shade under one of the seats and then put his line out. But he handed me his rod to hold, saying, "You hang onto it. I have to rig up a new leader for you. When those babies shoot out of the water and shake their jewelry at you, they sure do kink up the leader. This stiff wire snaps if it's badly kinked. Means a new leader half the time. Not that I mind," he added, grinning. He fixed Cappy with a gloating eye and said, "How do you like hardware by now? You better put those herring back in that aquarium you run."

"Day ain't over," Cappy answered complacently.

Soon all lines were out and we were trolling in the bay off Fishery Point. The water around us dimpled and bubbled as herring rose to the surface. Searching, greedy gulls rode the waves and made lightning darts at fish, quick and grabby as women at a rummage sale. They started their power dives several hundred feet up but braked with their wings as they neared the surface and lit on the water with hardly a ripple. Often they didn't touch the water before thrusting their curved, wicked beaks after the herring which was snatched at by another gull before the first one had time to swallow it. White birds, white mountains, and blue sea.

Over sandwiches and coffee, the men talked a fishing language I couldn't understand. I was contented but my companions wanted action. The motor droned on. Like a metronone, its rhythm was sensed but not actually heard. Loons flying overhead looked like ebony tenpins. Once in a while a salmon jumped, pivoted out of a circle of riffles, and slapped back into the water. All this peace must have bothered Cappy for he began to fidget; he spit, scratched his head, changed the water in the herring tub, and cleaned grass and seaweed off his line every few minutes. Finally he blurted out, "No use runnin' on a half head of steam. Gotta stoke the boiler." He found his bottle of gin—and satisfaction. After several noisy smacks, he wiped his mouth on the back of his hand, pushed his cap back, and mellowed into a reminiscent mood.

"Did I ever tell yuh about the shenanigan Sam Olsen pulled off? No? Well, once he had a helluva decision to make, had to do it in such a hurry that you can't blame the guy for choosin' wrong. Seems he took his mother-in-law out fishin' for kings in that twelve-foot dinghy he has. She was green as a June bride, never been fishin' before. They was trollin' off Parker's Reef on the north shore when a damn fool king that must have weighed fifty pounds hit her line. She hollered and 'bout fainted when the pole started bangin' around, so Sam took over. He played the b'jesus out of that fish—took him half an hour to git the starch out of his collar. But Sam finally got it up to the boat, gaffed it, and had it in.

"It was in the boat all right, but it was still as full of tricks as a trained nurse, thumpin' and heavin' around that little boat plenty. Sam was standin' up trying to knock it out when he lost his balance. He lurched against the starboard side and over went the whole shebang. Him and his maw sprawled out in the water like old Satchel Mouth had coughed 'em up, but Sam still had a hold of that pole. He grabbed the transom of the dinghy with his other hand and he could have pulled himself in. D'yuh know, Doc, I think he could have saved that fish if his fool mother-in-law hadn't yelled jest then. He had clean forgot her. When she screamed, what do yuh 'spose Sam did? He dropped that pole and grabbed the old woman. Saved her. But mebbe I'm too hard on him—he didn't have much time to think." Cappy spat and added thoughtfully, "Sam's a reasonably honest fisherman, says he's landed quite a few forty-pounders and this one had 'em all licked. Poor old Sam."

I was still laughing when Bill got a strike—and lost him. But either that salmon came back for a second taste or Bill hooked another. A moment later his line poured out and the tip of the vibrating rod marked its graph of success against the sky. Cappy Bell reeled his gear in to give Bill the field, hollering, "Slap her ears down, Doc. She's leadin' with her chin."

"Easy, Bill," I pleaded. "She's in an awful hurry. Must have just remembered why she's heading for the river."

"Well I'll make an old maid out of her yet," Bill grunted, tensed and fighting. My line was in and Cappy was just taking in the last few feet of his when he must have snagged a submarine. His line tore out. Two on at once!

"You keep that hellcat of yours away from my line or I'll—"

"You'll what?" Bill asked, winking at me. Cappy tapered off with a string of salty words and my head snapped from left to right as I cheered for both men. Bill reeled in almost to the boat four times. Each time the fish ran out again. It didn't seem possible Bill had a line on it when it jumped a hundred feet behind us, a silver flash that shot into the air and plopped back again. Finally Bill reeled in to his slip sinker. It slid down the line and there was the salmon, gasping beside the boat. He looked at me and nodded toward the net.

"Who? Me?" I was flabbergasted.

"Sure. You have to learn. Go under it easy. Get it head on. Don't get excited and jab at it—I'll lead it right into the net." I did just as he told me—with a few exceptions. Completely rattled, I stuck the net in the

water like I was harpooning a whale, scared the fish
crazy, and came up on his tail. He was in the net, his
head lolling over the rim, when something happened.
That silver shot out as if he had a spring in his tail. He
lashed his head from side to side, spit up the hook, and
was off.

"Bill! I'm so sorry. What happened?"

"Never mind, honey. That's just lesson number one.
You'll never net a salmon tail-on again. Forget it.
Watch Cappy handle his fish. He's plenty good."

Suffering pangs of remorse, I stood beside Cappy.
That old man knew the right things to tell a fish. He
coaxed it, threatened it, crooned and swore in its direction. His line never sagged for an instant yet he was
relaxed and unhurried. He was quick, cautious, and
sure, handling that rod like a maestro. When the salmon
was nearly in, it doubled back and knifed through the
water. Cappy hunched his shoulders and chuckled.
"Full of snoose, ain't she?"

He was using a large, free-running reel six inches in
diameter. It had two black nobs for handles which
blurred into a streak when line went out fast. He con-
trolled the flow of line by pressing his thumb on a
leather flap which snugged down on the spool, thus
slowing it as much or as little as he wished. I could see
this was a reel for an expert.

Cappy led the fish beside the boat, transferred the
pole to his left hand, and gently netted it with his right.
It looked so simple.

"Used a net just to show you how," he said to me.
"Generally I gaff 'em with this triple-hook setup. At
my age, I can't waste time unsnarlin' hooks wound up
in a net. Hand me the pipe."

While Bill helped him untangle the mess, I gazed longingly toward shore. That little sandy cove looked good to me, for my back ached and I wanted to stretch out on the beach.

"Tell you what," Cappy said, never missing a trick. "Suppose you go ashore and start bakin' that fish of yours in the sand. I'm hungry. I like somethin' to eat with my meals. Them razor-cut sandwiches you brought from the inn are wearin' mighty thin around the edges. Want to?"

I certainly did. It was after four o'clock and I was numb in that area closest to the hard board seat. Cappy worked the lumbering punt ashore, waded in, and tied the rope around a half-buried log on the beach. Bill and I gathered firewood from great piles of drift while Cappy cleaned my salmon with just a flash of his knife and an expert tug or two. A dozen sea gulls dropped down from nowhere and began playing tug-of-war with yards of fish guts. Finally, the old man sauntered over to us, holding the flattened silver by the gills.

"Here's a good place, far enough above high tide for a fire. Now dig a trench 'bout a foot deep but make it wider and longer than this fish. Doc, you build a fire in it, the hull length of it, while I show your wife how to wrap a fish in seaweed. There's a trick to it, but if it's done right, it'll be a sight better eatin' than anything you ever got in them plush and gilt places. Watch close."

He picked up a handful of fluggy green sea lettuce which he had gathered from the beach and wadded it against the salmon on both sides, binding it into place with ribbons of brown kelp, streamers three or four inches wide and ten feet long. He wound layer upon layer until the crisscrossed bandaged salmon resembled

an Egyptian mummy. When he had finished, he inspected the fire and turned to me, saying, "Listen real
careful. A lot of squaws have got kilt around here for
ruinin' a good salmon. Bill and I are goin' out fishin'
again and all you got to do is bake this salmon.

"Now just get this fire roarin' hot with plenty of
bark. Then let it burn down to coals that are hotter'n
hell. Next, cover the fire with about an inch of sand,
all over it. Lay the salmon on the thin layer of hot sand
and cover him up good with several more inches of
sand. Then build another fire on top of the fish and keep
stoking it till we get in. Got it?"

I got it—also a crick in my back from hauling wood,
and an assortment of splinters from the prickly fir bark.
Yet I loved tending that fire; even the smoke smelled
good. It was a golden, late-summer afternoon. The incoming tide lapped each rippling wave just a fraction
of an inch higher up the beach than the last one. The
cedars behind me whispered instead of rustling as leafy
trees do. A solitary sea gull, less timid than the rest,
hovered over the spot where the fish had been cleaned.
She was searching for odd tidbits. Bill had told me that
there was no way for the amateur to tell the sexes apart
as the males and females looked practically the same.
But I was sure this was a lady—she had such a feminine
way of ruffling and preening her feathers as she clucked
at me. And I chatted right back to her. Even on a
honeymoon, a little woman-talk is welcome. As I
watched the gull, something about her pigeon-toed,
fanny-waggling strut set me thinking. She was inde-
scribably graceful in the air, at home between clouds and
sea, and yet so clumsy on land. I decided it wasn't

cricket to judge anything or anyone out of his native environment—even Cappy.

Here we were in a wilderness but, as the crow is supposed to fly, only a dozen or so miles from the city of Bellingham. I could see the abrupt contrasts in this land of sea and mountains; places only a short distance apart differed dramatically. Bill had told me that the shore of the thundering Pacific or a lonely mountain snow field are only an afternoon's drive from Seattle. Perhaps one reason Westerners are such tolerant, uncritical people is because they are so diversified and have learned to respect one another's various abilities. The person living next door might be able to lead you to safety over a snow bridge above a glacier crevasse or another friend has what it takes to bring a boat through a raging storm. Still another can find his way in a dense forest.

My daydreamings were cut short by the staccato of the motor. First I heard it, then I saw it round Fishery Point, and later I smelled it as I ran down to meet the men coming ashore. Each proudly held up another salmon which had paid with its life for misjudging a herring.

Bill cleaned them while Cappy rummaged around in the boat and dragged out an ax and a carton which contained a loaf of bread, a can of coffee, a tin of milk, a blackened coffee pot, and a weird assortment of tin cups. These he placed upon a huge cast-up cedar stump near the fire. Then he picked up the ax, felt the blade with a cracked thumb, and swung it three times into another chunk of cedar, each swing slicing off a glassy smooth slab of wood.

"Plates," he explained. Then he kicked the burning logs off the fire and smothered the embers with sand.

"This unveiling is mighty damned important—unless you want to grind a new edge on your teeth with sand. Now watch me."

With a board, he carefully scraped the darkened, steaming sand off the top of the fish. When the wrappings of charred seaweed lay exposed, he slipped the board under the salmon and lifted it from its hot bed to the cedar table. The steam that drifted up would have graced high-grade ambrosia.

"Hey, Bill," he shouted, "old man Doucett won't mind if you git some water out of his well. It's over there under the maple close to the bank." Cappy had rebuilt the fire by the time Bill returned with the coffee pot full of water. My husband was beaming, exuberant; I'd never seen a person so satisfyingly happy.

Cappy said, "Now this is a perticular job. You have to brush the sandy seaweed off real easy or you'll cut through the skin and git sand into the meat. And it's hell-fire hot." With his knife, he flicked away the crisp seaweed, lifted it strand by strand, and pushed back the brittle inner wadding. Then he gently peeled the skin back, working from the belly to the backbone. There lay my fish. It was a gorgeous sunset pink without a speck of sand. It separated from the long, thin bones into moist and luscious looking chunks and it smelled divine. He heaped our cedar-slab plates and handed them to us before cutting the bread and pouring the coffee. Then he found himself a "leanin' log" and sat down in the sand, folding up in slow, creaky stages.

That fish! It was tender, juicy, and sweet with a delectable smoky tang. We ate it with our fingers and

it was the best I'd ever had in my life but I didn't waste
time talking about it. Bill's fork plied between plate and
mouth with assembly-line rhythm and Cappy, between
bites, smiled at us radiantly, smacking his lips. After
the mound on his slab had worked down a couple of
inches, he pushed our cups of coffee near us and inquired if we liked cream. When we nodded, he found
the can of milk. He jabbed two holes in it with his
knife, winked at me, and chanted:

> "No teats to pull,
> No hay to pitch
> Just punch a hole
> In the——can."

I chuckled along with the men; no post-Victorian
training could stand up under this. I'd never met anyone
like Cappy Bell; at this point I thought he was wonderful. Even his swearing was artistic. There was no malice
in his picturesque words, which rolled and reverberated
with good humor.

He helped us all to man-sized seconds of fish and this
he ate more slowly, tasting it critically. "Ain't bad.
S'good, but it ud be a damn sight better tomorrow.
Greenhorns don't know that all fish, 'cept mebbe trout,
is better if you rest it a while in a cool place. They think
the fresher fish is, the better it eats. Ain't true. If it's
aged a trifle, it don't stick to your teeth. Takes the
chewiness out of it. But this ain't too bad."

Nothing was bad in the whole wide world at this
moment. With our hat brims pulled down against the
brilliance of a sea turned gold we were watching the
lavender mist gather over the mountains. After a while,
we tossed our plates on the fire and just sat there, soak-

ing in the beauty of the sunset. No one spoke; evidently
the men had forgotten the long trip back to Orcas Island
which lay ahead of us. Twilight was deepening and I
knew we should start, but Cappy was stretched out on
one elbow with his feet to the fire.

"You know, Doc," he was saying, "this is a hot run
and it's no time to leave it. We could snag some more
silvers and mebbe pick up a king or two in the morning.
'Bout four-thirty, on the low slack. Fact is, we'll do it."

"Four-thirty!" I gasped. "We never could get back
here that early in the morning."

"I didn't say nuthin' about gettin' back. We're not
leavin'."

"You-mean-stay-overnight-here?" I was incredulous.

"Sure. Why not?"

"We can't possibly spend the night. No beds, no
clothes, not even any bedding. I'm going home."

"Told yuh, Bill," Cappy yawned. "It's a mistake to
take women on a fishin' trip. And if a woman insists
upon comin' along—"

"If you think I'm going to stay here all night and
freeze—"

"You won't freeze," Cappy drawled. "I got blankets
in the boat and you can wear your sheepskin coat. Guess
you never slept on a bed of hemlock branches. Best in
the world."

"No. And I don't intend to. Bill, let's get going."

"Now don't blow a gasket," Cappy said, not moving
an inch. "You just horned in on our party and I ain't
leavin' a mess of silvers out there to thumb their noses
at us. When fishing's good yuh might as well stick with
it and fish."

"Cappy," Bill began diplomatically, "perhaps we better had—"

"Turn in," he spoke with finality. "We're stayin' and four o'clock in the morning's right after dinner."

"We really should go," Bill said reluctantly, glancing uneasily at me. He can be very convincing when he wants to, but he certainly wasn't putting his all into this.

"Tell you, Doc," Cappy said, getting up, "you got a lot to learn about women. They's just like salmon—give 'em a slack line and they'll make a fool out of yuh every time." He ambled down to the boat and brought back his vile-looking blankets which he dumped at my feet. I recoiled as though he had hit me; the rich, ripe aroma of countless generations of herring rose up in a sickening wave. Mother had taught me that a lady never is surrounded by anything worse than an unpleasant odor; delicacy would not permit the word "stink." But these blankets stunk. Bill did have the grace not to look at me as he contemplated the unsavory pile between us. He was thoughtfully pulling at his lower lip and muttering about how this wasn't his idea, and how sorry he was and how Cappy was a stubborn cuss.

The old man had left us; he was at the water's edge, untying the boat. He beckoned to Bill, waited until he was near, and then said, "Git in the boat and pull the anchor out from under the rear seat." He waited while Bill did it. "I'm goin' to show yuh an old Siwash trick. Learned it from Indian George. How to anchor a boat so the tide won't get it—but you can. And without usin' a dinghy, either.

"Now, Bill, we ain't got a prow so coil the anchor chain on a seat. Do it real careful so it will pay out without catchin'."

I stepped out of smelling distance of the blankets and watched; a woman never is so mad that she isn't curious. Now Cappy Bell was in the boat and was tying one end of a long rope on a fluke of the anchor which was balanced carefully on the gunwale. With the coil of rope in hand, Cappy motioned Bill to follow him ashore. He picked up a long, stout pole and then waded out as far as he could without shipping water in his hip boots. Then, with one end of the pole butted into the back of the boat, he gave it a tremendous shove seaward. The rope with one end attached to the anchor, payed out. When the punt had drifted as far as it would go, Cappy jerked the rope. This pulled the anchor off the gunwale and it splashed overboard. The crazy craft now was anchored beyond the reach of low tide and Cappy had a line on it.

"See, Bill? Slicker'n a flounder's belly. I'll tie this end of the rope here on shore and in the morning I can lift the anchor easy 'cause the pull will be direct on the fluke while the boat tugs against the anchor and the chain." He spit reflectively and added, "It'll hold—short of a nor-easter, and we don't git them hellbusters in summer. Git the ax and follow me."

I was alone. From the spooky black trees which edged the beach there was the sound of slashing as trees were stripped of their lower branches for bough beds. The fire had been extinguished and it was nearly dark. The stars were faint in the gray-black sky but they seemed to dance as I looked at them. I was mad clear through. Because I couldn't do anything else, I decided to be icily remote and aloof. But I spoiled it all by shrieking when a bat zoomed out of the woods straight at me. Bill came tearing to my side, but I told him haughtily to go back to his friend, that he didn't need to concern himself over me at all. He hastily departed, leaving me alone again on that scary beach. Goose pimples ran in waves all over me. This was a fine way to spend the last night of our honeymoon.

Most infuriating was the sound of Bill and Cappy chatting together, happy as gulls at low tide. Above the insistent lap-lap of the waves, there was the rustle of evergreen branches being piled into beds, and I caught snatches of conversation. Cappy was saying something about how I would simmer down in the morning and that a couple of runs always took the fight out of even the biggest ones. Bill did not answer.

Kicking at stones in my path, I stalked over to the men and glowered down at the least inviting beds I'd ever seen.

"You'll think you're smack in the middle of a cloud when you hit this," Cappy crooned softly, adding a last fluffy branch to the tailored pile which was to be mine.

"Ever sleep out under the moon before, darling?" Bill asked, unctuously. I shook off the arm he slipped around me.

"I tell yuh, Bill, you're forgettin'," Cappy said, placing a fatherly hand on my husband's shoulder. "What do yuh do when a big king logs down and won't budge? Why, you leave it alone for a spell. Kinda cools it off if you don't jerk the line. Let's turn in." He tossed a blanket on each of the bough beds and let himself down creakily on the one furthest away.

Not looking at either of them, I flopped down on my stack of branches. Bill considerately pulled my blanket up over me but I hastily kicked it off as ghosts of herring rose up around me. Silently, Bill went to his own bed,

and almost immediately twin snores hacked at my
nerves. Even snuggled down in my heavy coat, I was
cold. So, with loathing, I reached for the encrusted
blanket, hating everything that swims. No matter how I
turned and twisted, butt ends of branches worked
through the fir needles. There was no escaping them.
Aching in every muscle, I lay on one side until I felt
like a pin cushion and then tried the other, wishing I
might have a strangle hold on some of the authors I'd
read who drooled about the ecstacy "of sleeping on a bed
of fragrant pine boughs." Had sand fleas hopped in their
faces and moonlight pried under their eyelids? Now I
knew how those Hindu martyrs felt when they slept on
a bed of nails.

Then in some dreamy place a million miles away, sea
gulls were screaming. My face felt warm. I opened my
eyes, not believing I'd ever been asleep. Sunshine!
Fearing my back would snap, I sat up gingerly and
looked about. The men's beds were empty and the boat
out of sight. But weighted under a stone beside me was
a message scrawled on the back of a leader-wire en-
velope: "Gone to catch breakfast. Be back soon. De-
votedly, Bill." Four matches were stuck through the
paper and the coffee pot was full of water.

So they expected me to make a fire! I'd show them I
was no squaw. I heaved that blanket as far as I could
and ran down the beach, surveying the brand-new day.
Surprisingly enough, I felt wonderful and must have
slept for hours, as it was after ten o'clock. The water
was 'way out and a magic low-tide wonderland steamed
in the sun. Morning, with its brightness and gaiety, got
into my blood, and the warm, firmly packed sand felt

good to my bare feet. Wandering about, I found a fairy-tale sort of pool cupped behind a boulder. The water was deliciously warm. Soon, clothes thrown helter-skelter, I was lying in it, tingling with pleasure and the exuberance one finds at the end of a quest. Never had I been outdoors before with no human beings near by, and though I knew people lived on Waldron Island, there were no signs of habitation. Bill had told me that George Vancouver had discovered the San Juan Islands in 1792, and it looked as though no one had been back since.

The little crystal pool was a prism of enchantment, a tiny marine world. I found horny purple starfish wedged under the rock, tightly attached by hundreds of vacuum cups. Under the surface of the water bloomed red and feathery flowers which shot back into their tubes when I touched them. That almost inaudible clicking sound came from the barnacles as they opened and closed. They were stuck end-wise on the rock and they reminded me of bleached, salted pistachio nuts. Baby crabs skuttled sideways under cover of green sea lettuce. If I held my fingers still for a long time, tiny fish swam between them and the hermit crabs came out of the homes they had stolen. There were all manner of shells: small rosy pink ones, larger hinged shells with Indian-basket designs on them, and little squatty cones that gleamed like opals in the sunshine. Deciding I wanted an evening gown the lovely blue-purple of mussel shells reminded me of clothes, so I rolled out of the pool onto the hard sand. Soon I was dry, lightly powdered all over with a film of dried salt.

I had left more in that pool than the imprint of my body. A lot of habits were dissolved; it had been my

baptism into the congregation of those who love life
over and above its inconveniences. Dressing, I breathed
deep, for the air smelled of salt and seaweed and cedar
in the sun.

There was barely time to get a fire going under the
coffee pot before I heard the motor. But big steam bubbles were exploding through the coffee grounds by the
time the men came ashore. Only Cappy threw fish on
the sand, three huge ones, and I knew he had made his
point. A fresh herring could lick a tin spoon.

Bill waved to me, a little uncertainly. Even from that
distance I felt his eyes searching mine. There were
words I had to eat before I could tackle breakfast; there
wasn't a thing I could shout to him, so I slipped a stick
through two corners of my handkerchief and ran
toward him down the beach, carrying my flag of truce.
When he threw his arms around me, I didn't mind the
fish scales on his shirt nor the smell of the boat behind
him. I didn't even mind Cappy Bell's crack when he
looked at us and grunted, "Told you, Bill. They may
throw kinks in the leader but an old hand can snub 'em
in every time. She's learnin'."

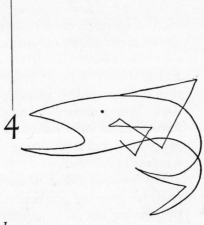

4

Babies, bottles, and bass

I still was learning—two babies, seven years, and ten pounds later—learning how to soothe anxious patients on the telephone, how to trace a busy physician from call to call, and how to reheat fish for his unpredictable dinner hour. Exuberantly happy, I wallowed in maternity; the only eternal triangle in my life was folded and stacked on top of the others. For Bob was welcomed into the family before "Cookie's" diapers were dry. That was the nickname we had for our elder son, Bill junior, and we gave it to him partly because of our name and to avoid the confusion of two "Bills" and also because that cunning little boy had great melted-chocolate eyes.

Bill fairly adored the two boys and we all had a rollicking good time together but, with babies eighteen months apart, there were moments when I thought my spring wardrobe should include a strait jacket. I envied those complacent oriental gods who have a hundred hands. Never did two children have a bigger head of steam. They rode wagons down the cellar steps, swallowed poison, filched the neighbor's jam, and flushed all manner of sundries down the toilet. Even before they approached the baseball age, we paid for nearly every window in our block.

My husband fished whenever he could sneak away from his growing practice. Often I hopefully planned to go along but some juvenile gland or other backfired and I had to stay at home. I hated being a fishing-widow but the edge of my hatred was dulled by the fish, which we were mighty glad to have as we unfortunately built our Seattle home in 1929. Bill swore it was building this house which touched off the world's worst depression. At any rate, like most of our friends, we were nipped in the budget. But we could always eat the fish that Bill brought back from numerous one-day trips.

About the time our sons shifted from diapers to training panties, Bill insisted fishing should become a family affair. So Cookie and Bob were literally brought up in the wet end of a boat, and they loved everything pertaining to fish. Their father certainly had dug down deep in his genes for these embryonic fishermen. They played with trout instead of tin soldiers and had hardly dropped rattles before learning to steer our new outboard motor.

I discovered a few things about that motor myself—that a bobbie pin should be included with the tools and that a woman's delicate touch really is excellent when it comes to cleaning that wisp of a filter. Bill was unimpressed and explained it logically by saying motors must be feminine because they respond only to loving, understanding treatment and raise hell when they're abused.

When the boys were pre-school age, we took them to Mission Beach one day for salmon trout. They had been fishing with Bill before and had gone through all the motions but never had landed any fish. I was lukewarm about this trip for I knew what would happen. I'd be forgotten and relegated to the prow of the boat while the "men" fished. And this, after I'd packed the tackle and enough lunch for The Four Horsemen, as well as tending two hot, sticky little boys.

We drove to Mission Beach, hired a boat, and started off—all while the September sun was trying to fry us alive. Sure enough, Bill suggested I "relax" up forward, on a seat ten inches wide. Soon the motor droned like a great dragonfly and Bill helped *his* sons put out their hand lines. They always were his sons when they were clean and behaving. Pop gear and worms sank behind them.

Exhausted, I slumped down and went over that last hurried hour in the kitchen. No, I hadn't forgotten a thing this time: salt for the hard-boiled eggs, sugar for our coffee, and a thermos of milk for the boys. Food. Perhaps the heat was making me giddy but it seemed I was eternally swimming in a sea of calories, afloat on an ocean of barley soup, with a bit of meat here and a log of celery there, and the fish were the elusive vitamins. Eyes closed, my mind wandered back to the boys' baby days. Just as plainly as I recalled their first steps, I remembered the pounds of prunes I had strained. If the carrots I had sieved were laid tip to top, very likely they would circle the earth. When Cookie yelled, I opened my eyes with a start.

Cookie had a fish on! The boys were in their bathing trunks and two brown-velvet bodies were bending over the hand lines. Bill was standing up behind them, smiling down like a benevolent Buddha. It was ridiculous, those babies fishing. But there was no doubt about it: Cookie had a trout. He winced as the stout, twisted line burned his finger when the fish ran out. It must have been an hereditary instinct that made him play it so well. Bill netted it and the boat rocked with joy. The pop gear flashed out again. We must have been in a mile-wide school of trout for the lines were hardly wet again before both boys hooked fish. More trout came in and the "men" were practically incoherent.

Now I was all attention. I looked at our five- and six-year-old children as though I'd never seen them before. These weren't my babies; here were two useful people who could do things for themselves. Clutching hands could hold, now. Starry-eyed, they scrambled up to the prow and proudly handed me their precious fish. Four nice trout, enough for dinner tomorrow night! For the first time in their lives, they were helping us and not asking for something. Eagerly, I reached for their fish. They were symbols to me—my first returns from prunes and carrots.

This trip was a shot in the arm to the boys—not that they needed it—and they put the salmon bite on us all week to take them again. The following Sunday we might have gone back to Mission Beach for more juvenile trout, except Bill heard that blackmouth were hitting at Holmes Harbor. Big fifteen-pounders were being landed by spinning, so he made a proposition to his sons.

He explained that this fishing was too complicated for little boys, but we would take them along and let them use their hand lines for trout later in the day. He promised, that is, if they'd let us spin undisturbed for a while. It was a deal with much handshaking.

Sunday morning we got up early and, while I was packing the eternal lunch, Bill made rounds at the hospitals. I hoped I wasn't jumping the gun; I'd been disappointed so often that now I seldom let my hopes get up until I saw the whites of his eyes. Cookie and Bob were out digging worms and they had a pailful, enough to tempt every trout north of San Francisco. They stopped only long enough to wave shovels at their father as he drove into the garage.

When Bill entered the kitchen, he had that very-sick-patient look I knew so well. I gazed at the boys, the lunch hamper, and the stack of tackle and sighed.

"Oh, we're still going," he said thoughtfully, "but that patient with a broken back feels uneasy this morning. It's probably just the pressure of his cast. I've left the telephone number of the fishing resort with the intern. I could be back in an hour. Get in the car, kids."

The ferry ride from the mainland to Whidby Island was beautiful and the trip to Holmes Harbor would have been nice except the bucket of worms tipped over. I knew we'd be finding them in the car for days. At the resort, we rented a boat and Bill started rowing. Just for fun we all flipped a coin to see who would be "captain for the day," this after some heavy masculine discussion as to whether one of my sex should be allowed to participate. Cookie and Bob were disgusted when I won and signed them on as lowly junior officers. Bill was first mate.

Looking sternly at them, I warned, "Any mutiny, men, and I'll throw you in the brig. Unless you keep out of our way up in the prow, I'll put you in irons. And—"

"Isn't this about right, Captain?" Bill asked, shipping his oars. "There's a feeding shoal all along here. We can try 'most any place." While he heaved out the anchor, I gazed about the protected harbor cupped out of the wooded shore. We were only a few hundred yards from the beach and had company around us. Not very far away was round little fir-clad Baby Island, surrounded by more fishermen in rowboats. The boys were contented on the decked-over bow; with their shoes and stockings off they were splashing their feet in the water, kicking at jellyfish and splashing each other.

From a bucketful of water, Bill picked up one of the big free-running reels with its well-soaked raw silk line. Two clear, bluish leaders floated on top.

"I wish some wise guy would invent a clear line that doesn't kink when it's dry. These have to be soaked. Now these are Tegusa leaders, from Japan. I sorted over a couple of dozen before I found these strong, clear ones." He attached the heavy ends of the tapered leaders to the swivels on three-ounce crescent sinkers. The other end of the sinker was fastened to the main line, after it had been threaded through the guides of the pole. I was glad these poles were cheap because they were ten feet long and made of very limber bamboo.

"There," Bill said, laying the poles down and reaching for a board. "Now I'll show you how to cut spinners. Watch me." He sharpened his knife to a razor edge and cut a pennant-shaped fillet from each side of a six-inch herring. The knife cut up toward the skin as it neared the tail of the spinner to give it more flutter. The top, cut just below the gills, was beveled at an angle and he snipped a tiny triangle off the thick point of the top.

"For luck?" I asked.

"Nope. Makes it spin better." He held it up admiringly.

"Looks like a three-inch herring, doesn't it?" he said.

"Why not save yourself some trouble and *use* a whole small fish?" I never would understand fishermen.

" 'Cause these cut spinners are better. More flexible so they twirl and flash. It's the diagonal pull on this firm bevel that makes 'em spin in the water. Though I've used candlefish and had luck with them, too. Sometimes they like one thing, sometimes another. But more times salmon like spinners."

He showed me how to bait our number two hooks. The point went through the top of the spinner, through the thick edge on the skin side. Then he worked it back through the skin again with a twisting motion so that the point and barb of the hook were exposed through the skin and lay lengthwise of the spinner.

"Some men use a drop hook, often a triple-gang hook, that swings free a few inches below the main hook. I don't think it spins quite so well, but if we start losing fish we'll put them on. Let's go. Here's your pole."

Bill showed me how to hold the pole with my right hand and wedge the butt securely under my arm. Then he told me how to cast, to let the spring of the rod snap the bait out. Line fell off the reel easily. When the lead hit the water and had taken the spinner down, he demonstrated how to strip the line in with my left hand with steady, arm-length pulls. It coiled beside

me in the bottom of the boat. I held the line gently between two felt finger protectors worn on my right
thumb and forefinger.

"Hold your line easy," Bill cautioned. "As a rule, fish
strike when the line is not moving, when the bait is at
rest. The trick is to have the spinner alternately flash
and lie quiet." He explained what would happen to my
ten-pound test leader if a fish hit while I was clamping
down hard on the line. I got the picture.

"When do I use my reel—or is it just for looks?" I
asked, motioning the children away from my coil of line
in the bottom of the boat.

"You play the fish on the reel. His first run usually
takes out all the free line."

We fished for quite a while and my stripping arm was
tired. My line was coiled beside me and I was set to
make a honey of a cast. The lead flew out—and then
there was a terrible howl from Cookie.

"Look what you're doing!" Bill snapped at me as he
picked up the crying child. "That's what happens when
you step on the line in the boat. When you cast and
it can't go out, of course it flies back and somebody's
apt to get hit. Keep your big foot off the line."

I was so sorry about my clumsiness that I let the "first
officer" use my pole. I thought he could catch as many
fish as I could. I was convinced Father Neptune himself
could not have found one with a search warrant.

Bill fooled me. Just then his coil of line flew out
through the guides and soon more was pouring off the
reel.

"Fish on!" he shouted. "It's a honey and full of gin
and jamboree. Make way for a prince."

"What do you mean, Daddy? What's a prince?"

"Well, a blackmouth is a college-age king. A green one. Wouldn't that make him a prince?" Slowly, carefully he brought it in, tensed for his first surprise run. The pole often dipped to the water and I could see that half the fun of spinning lay in the lightness of the tackle used. It's brain, not brawn, that counts here.

Then that fish jumped.

"Man, oh man," Bill chanted, "blackmouth don't jump. It's a hooknose silver. That's the real McCoy."

"Daddy," Bob implored seriously, "don't let McCoy get away."

The line was rippling through the water when suddenly it cut toward the bow, as though the devil was after it.

"Shall I start praying for the leader to hold?"

"No. Get that anchor rope up in a hurry." His line was slack now. I was gingerly stepping over my own coil on the floorboards when I saw a man rowing toward us. He looked like the resort owner but I didn't have time for another glance. Bill was in plenty of trouble. His line had jerked to a stop. Now it wouldn't come in an inch. Just as I had my hands on the anchor rope, Cookie leaned over the side and said, "Mommie, McCoy's down here."

I peered through the greenish water and saw a beautiful big salmon winding the leader around the anchor rope. He was going round and round in a Maypole dance. Of course Bill knew what had happened but I was grateful he was not talkative about it. While I was wondering what he would do, I saw the fish snap the leader and frisk away. Before I could say anything, the man in the boat yelled at us, "Hey, Doctor, you're wanted on the telephone. Call long-distance operator 46."

We just looked at each other.

Silently Bill reeled in his empty line and I cast my coiled line so as to bring it back on the reel. The officers were stricken.

"What about our trout, Daddy? Remember you promised."

"I know. I'm awfully sorry. We'll see." Bill rowed in, beached the boat, and hurried to the telephone. When he returned, he said to me, "Let's pack. We're leaving." I helped him without flicking an eyelash. Doctors' wives get numb to the prods of disappointment and develop a sort of Far East philosophy of their own.

"Is it the patient in the body cast?" I inquired.

"Yes. Sounds like he has appendicitis—and it's a heck of a time to have it."

"I'll say it is," Cookie cut in vehemently, "when you *promised* we could—"

"What'll you do?"

"Operate, if I have to." He ran his fingers through his hair, adding, "It won't be easy working through a window cut in that full-length body cast. The patient recovered from a flare-up several years ago and I hope he can weather it this time. But I doubt it from what the intern reported. Said his white-cell count was up to ten thousand now."

We drove to the ferry in silence. On the mainland, Bill stepped on the gas and we fairly flew back to Seattle. He went directly to the hospital and asked us to wait in the car until he returned. Minutes dragged into half an hour. Finally the unhappy and restless boys spotted their father coming toward us. He was worried.

"I'm staying. They are getting the surgery ready now. It's appendicitis all right. Blood count's 'way up, no chance of putting it off. You go on home." He looked down at his sons hanging on his arms and said gently, "I'm going to keep my promise. Would you settle for a whole week's fishing trip on Orcas Island next spring?" Their whoops of joy drew glances from the tight-faced Sunday visitors entering the hospital. He patted my shoulder and left. As I watched him walk away, a great hurting lump rose in my throat.

Time marched on and so did the boys. As the winter skimmed by, hardly a week passed but that one of the boys reminded his father of the promised trip to Orcas, always specifying that it be one without an appendix.

And then, *finally*, June came and the exciting evening when Bill brought home two short, steel fishing rods for the boys. Their screams of delight rose to heaven when he handed each child his own tackle box. The wrapping paper was snatched off and thrown to the floor where Bonnie, our cocker spaniel puppy, promptly shredded it to bits. Alternately, they hugged their father and the new tackle.

"Now, Cookie," Bill said, "let's wind this new cuttyhunk line from these spools onto your reel." Father and son went to work. Even in the living room it wasn't safe to let the line fall slack because as soon as it dipped down, the kittens would bat at it. Felix and Felina were adorable little fluffballs, near-Persian, and they had a field day pawing at the line.

"Fellas, d'you think you could be ready to leave this next Saturday? Cabin's all reserved." There was worse pandemonium when they heard this, but I couldn't enjoy their pleasure since a most distressing thought had just come to me. Bob's tonsils! We had planned his tonsillectomy for mid-June as the physician we wanted to do the operation was leaving town for the summer.

By main force, I dragged Bill from the living room and reminded him. It did take some of his bounce away for a moment. Reservations were hard to get by now and he had planned his work so he could be away that week. After some discussion, we agreed to have the tonsillectomy done immediately, even though Bob would have only a few days in which to recuperate before we left for the Islands. I was a bit reluctant, but Bill said the salt air and sunshine would fix him up in no time. Anyway, Bill would be with the boy and Bob was as husky as a Roman gladiator and of somewhat the same temperament.

Bob stood the operation better than I did. Two days later it was hard keeping him quiet while I sorted and packed for the trip. We had decided it would be easier on Bob if he and I took the excursion boat instead of going by car with Bill and Cookie. The man from whom we were renting the cabin would meet us at the dock.

Saturday dawned drizzling and dripping; the clouds were down to our shoetops. We wore slickers to pack in the car a vast assortment of fishing gear, cooking utensils, dishes, bedding, outboard motor, canned food, suitcases, and lastly, our "zoo." Bill wasn't a bit pleased at the prospect of taking the pup and the kittens, but I gave him a leash for the former and a sand box for the latter and told him a father's life can't be all skittles and beer. He balked, saying he wasn't going to have any damned carpenter cats chewing his ears on an eighty-mile drive.

"Carpenter cat? What do you mean?"

"They're the kind that do odd jobs around the house. I won't take them." Just then Bob climbed into the car, picked up both kittens, and hugged them to him. Looking at us with great limpid eyes underlined with violet shadows, he appeared deceptively angelic. He was still pale but beneath his quivering lips the set of his jaw warned his father.

Bill grunted something, shook his head, and crossed his fingers for luck. He drove Bob and me to the dock. At the gangplank, I kissed them both good-by and implored Bill not to let that last call at the hospital keep him from making the morning ferry at Anacortes. I asked him to pick up something for dinner that night in the cabin. As the ship pulled out, he and Cookie waved but soon they were lost to sight in the rain. At the moment, I thought I had the long end of the deal.

Bob was fretful during the six-hour boat trip for his throat was still on fire. He wouldn't lie down and he climbed over everything. He cried to go on deck but the weather was too damp and bone-chilling. Fog, like soggy cotton, obscured a land which looked as if it had taken the veil for its sins. The melancholy boom of the fog horns along the coast had the persistency of an aching tooth, and only close to the ship's side could I see the water which was flat and oily, as uninteresting as a pail of gray paint. Bob wailed. He begged for food and I had to feed him promises of the hot soup we'd have soon after we landed. We had figured that Bill should arrive at the cabin about the same time we would.

Finally, when both Bob and I were worn out, he nestled in my lap and we watched the gulls sweep past the window. The birds looked like fragments of the gray fog; their mournful cries set my teeth on edge.

The boat was late docking at East Sound on Orcas Island. It was well after one o'clock. There was no one to meet us so I carried Bob down the wharf to the lawn of the inn where Bill and I had spent our honeymoon. We huddled under a covered lawn swing while we waited for the man to meet us. I tried to telephone but the line was out of order. I tried leaving Bob by the fire in the inn, but he yowled when I left him to watch for our man with the car.

By two o'clock, Bob had drooped off to sleep. The mist had bristled into a rain. Half starved, I daydreamed about that snug little cabin of peeled logs in a hemlock thicket. I'd never seen one but that was the way it always looked in *House and Garden.* Now I began to fume at Bill. If he'd caught the eleven o'clock ferry, he must be there by now and why wasn't he out looking for me?

In the distance, I heard a series of junior-grade explosions which gradually became louder as a rattletrap car came into sight. It had been a sedan in the first flush of its mechanical youth, but now old age had robbed it of its top and rear seat. Something in the car was squawking and squealing. The driver, genial as could be, waved to us and brought the car to a chattering stop. I asked him to wait a moment while I returned the blanket and untouched food I had begged for Bob. He had been too upset to eat it. I picked the child up, brushed off the pneumonia germs, and got in the front seat beside the man.

"Been here long?" he asked, racing the tired engine which longed to die. "I was aimin' to work on the car all week, and today 'bout one o'clock when I started out to git yuh, she popped a fan belt. Had to sew it up with a darnin' needle. An' while I was near Jake's place, thought I might as well pick up these here pigs. Took time."

I was relieved to know that the sacks bumping and thumping in back held pigs and not disembodied spirits. The car shuddered through the gears and we jerked off. We drove a few miles along tree-lined country roads but scenery is no good on an empty stomach. I was having a very personal feud with the broken wire springs which protruded through the seat covers. Chuck holes were something to worry about. Finally we entered a heavily wooded stretch where branches of fir, sagging with the weight of the rain, brushed our heads. I was soaked by the time he applied the protesting brakes.

"Here we are. If you want anything, just holler. I'm going down to the beach and caulk my boat. Should have done it last year." With that he goaded the engine and the car creaked out of sight.

There it stood, our "log cabin." The walls were made of a few scraggly slabs of bark tacked over unpainted boards. There was a tar-paper roof, and rain wept off the eaves. The chimney and the porch leaned to starboard and were threatening to topple over and call it a day. It was the sorriest-looking shack I'd ever seen and it was completely swallowed up by drooping, dripping cedar trees. Worst of all, our car wasn't there so Bill must have missed the morning ferry. Now it would be seven o'clock before he could get here.

I carried Bob into the one room—and nearly dropped him. So this was to be our home for a week. It was the gloomiest place this side of Wuthering Heights. Gray light came through two small, dirty windows. In the gloaming, I could see one table, three chairs, and a mattress on sagging springs. In one corner was a mean-looking wood stove which blended into the black tar-paper walls. Over the chipped sink was a shelf holding a kerosene lamp, a left-over box of corn flakes, and a cake of mouse-nibbled soap. Pink.

I rolled Bob onto the naked mattress which appeared to need rest more than we did. As I covered him with my coat, he wakened and cried for a drink. Holding his mouth up close to the faucet, I turned it on but there was only a dismal, rusty trickle.

Putting him off as best I could, I fell into the hollow of the mattress, pulled the damp coat over both of us, and finally went to sleep. I dreamed I had died of starvation and gone to hell. A sudden sly, rustling noise wakened me. Rising up on my elbow, I listened closely. It seemed to come from the shelf. Again that dry rattle, and the box of corn flakes jiggled a little and gave forth a horrible little squeak. There was a mouse in those corn flakes!

He could have 'em—I didn't want anything in the place. I have a shuddery loathing for the creepy things and I wouldn't have touched that box if the Kohinoor diamond was inside with a gift card attached. Shivering, I pulled the coat over our heads and prayed that the mouse would stay there.

It was almost dark when a blast from the horn of our car jerked me upright in bed. I was crawling out of the hole in the mattress when Cookie dashed in. "Mother," he shrilled, "what d'you think? The captain let me steer the ferry boat! Where's Bob? And guess what Daddy brought for dinner?"

Then Bill bounced into the cabin, with kittens and pup in one arm and a carton of canned food in the other. "Hi, darling. See you made out okay. How's Bob?" He was beaming.

"What? No fire?" He set the kittens down, scooted Bonnie across the floor, and playfully poked his son in the ribs. "Let's get a fire going for that surprise we have for Mother. Here, Cookie, you crumple the paper and I'll get kindling. It's nasty out today but it will be fine tomorrow. Great to be here."

"Just great," I answered through clenched teeth.

Whistling with what I thought was uncalled-for jocularity, he went out and returned with a fistful of wet kindling and a package he tossed to me. "Here we are. It'll taste mighty good. That steak I had on the ferry didn't seem to stick to my ribs." He lit the fire which promptly went out and belched smoke and charred paper back into his face. I didn't blame that stove. I'd act the same if I had to spend all my life in this cabin. Cookie, on tiptoe, was tugging at my arm, begging me to open the bundle.

I unwrapped the paper and there lay a naked chicken with its revolting limp neck dangling in mid-air. A half-closed eye stared back at me in icy hatred. No one had tampered with its vitals.

"Um. Roast chicken," Bill said, licking his lips. Only a long line of steady New England ancestors stayed my hand, for I itched to wrap that bird around his neck. Instead, I dropped it resoundingly on the table and ominously grabbed a couple of cans of beans out of the carton.

In the morning, I opened my eyes, looked around the

bleak hut, and then pinched them tight shut again. Rain
was pounding on the roof, long-drop rain that dribbled
down the window panes and left crooked little alleys in
the dirt. Bob was heavy as lead in the hollow of the
mattress beside me but Bill was stamping around on the
lean-to porch where he had slept. From the window I
saw the weeping firs against a gray, desolate sky. That
same gray, ten shades deeper, permeated the room. In
the cold half-light, Bill came in with a load of dripping
kindling.

"Good morning, dear," he said guardedly. Then, as-
suming a hearty tone which wouldn't have fooled an
idiot, he said, "This will be a different place when I get
the lamp lighted and this old stove roaring. Cookie's
still asleep in the car. Where's the bacon?"

My clothes were so damp that my teeth chattered as I
dragged them on—it was like sliding naked into a bed of
moss. I hung Bob's clothes by the fire, half expecting to
find them fuzzy with green mold. Bill's determined
cheerfulness didn't help one bit, but I was relieved when
Bob popped out of bed spry as a fingerling trout. Just
then, Cookie stumbled into the room, leaving barefoot
tracks of mud and brown fir needles. The kittens
pounced on the sleeping bag he had dragged through
the puddles. Another item to dry by the stove.

During breakfast, the rain really shifted into high and
pelted the windows so hard that the drops bounced back.
Driving rain on a tar-paper roof is unbelievably noisy;
it was like living inside a kettledrum.

After we had finished eating, both boys wanted to go
fishing. Bill took Bob on his lap and spoke to him gently.
"Sorry, fella, but you can't go out today in all this rain.
You're not well enough yet. You and Mother will have

to play in the house while Cookie and I get some cod. Too bad, honey, I know it's tough."

"I'll say it is," I blurted out. "It looks like a dandy day for me." Of course Bob cried and I thought I would scream if I saw one more drop of water. Instead, I heated milk for the kittens and did the breakfast dishes while Bill and Cookie donned slickers, boots, and sou'-wester hats. They were going to town for milk and cod gigs. It took much backing and maneuvering to slither the car out of the mud.

After they had left, I wrapped a still whimpering Bob in my raincoat and carried him to the backhouse. Now some of these contraptions are privies—and some are just plain backhouses. This model was definitely the latter. There was no path to it and none was needed; one could find it blindfold at midnight. I shoved the sagging door open. Bob clung to my hand desperately as he teetered on the edge of the seat. The walls were tiled in green moss and the catalogue was clammy and limp as I picked it up. The harness section stuck to the ladies' corsets.

"Mommie," Bob wailed, "I don't mind the smell so much, but it makes my eyes sting." As I sloshed back to the house, my already great admiration for pioneers was strengthened. I was thinking of their unheralded reserves of fortitude. No wonder they could lick the Indians.

In the cabin I found the kittens hissing at each other over the chicken on the drain board. The paper around it was shredded but the bird was still intact. I was tempted to hurl the ugly thing down the bank to the beach below. Then I recalled how women in slick magazine stories always found surcease from their troubles by cooking. They tie on organdy aprons, whip up a

fluffy cake, and magically their world adjusts itself. I
didn't think it would work but I'd give it a whirl. However, when I remembered that the bird would have to be
drawn before I could cook it, I felt more like a heroine
in a dour Russian novel. Cleaning a chicken was a closed
book to me—and I should have left it that way. Shuddering, I tackled the job, recalling the page in my cook-
book where Fannie Farmer does it so easily, and finally
shoved a denuded bird in the oven and slammed the
door shut.

An hour later, Bill drove up, skidded to a stop, and
Cookie came bounding in the door. "Hey, Mommie.
Guess what? The store didn't have any cod gigs, so
Daddy and I are going to make some. Won't that be
fun?" I reserved my opinion. Bill came in loaded down
with groceries, tackle box, and tool kit he had brought
from the car. On the table he laid four sections of copper pipe, each about four inches long. Then he shucked
out of his dripping oilskin coat, glanced obliquely at me,
and must have decided a kiss wouldn't help. He lit the
lamp, told Cookie to get the fire red hot and to put the
can of solder on the warmest place.

I held Bob in my lap to keep him off the drafty floor.
We watched Bill take heavy cuttyhunk line and stout
wire from his kit. He cut four pieces of wire about five
inches long.

"Now watch, fellas. I'm going to twist the ends of
this wire together, leaving a loop at the top. Like this.
The line goes through that loop which will stick out of
the top of the gig." He told us that cod were easy to
catch. They are such darned fools that they strike at
anything shiny, especially if it's moving.

"Don't need any bait. They're awfully dumb—maybe

that's why they're never in schools. Solder melted yet, Cookie?"

The stove was looping along and we all had to move back from the heat.

"Do cod look like salmon?" I asked.

"Frankly...no. They've never won any blue ribbons for beauty but they are good eating. Being morons doesn't seem to hurt the flavor. Cod's not as rich and good as salmon. But they are here, which silvers and kings are not. At the store, Karl Templin told me that there aren't many salmon around yet. Seem to be late this year."

He was upending the four pieces of copper pipe on a board, steadying each section with pliers as he poured in the molten solder. Then he quickly inserted the twisted wires in each, the loops exposed at the top. Soon the solder hardened and he tossed the four of them into a pail of cold water. When they were cool enough to handle, he drilled a hole through each solder-filled pipe at the end opposite from the wire loop and threaded lengths of cuttyhunk line through the holes. Next he slipped a *shiny* triple hook on each piece of line and tied the ends so that the hook swung free just below the bottom of the gig.

"Now," he said, beaming. "Get the idea? The solder makes this pipe heavy enough to sink rapidly. But the main thing is to shine up the copper so it will gleam and attract our simple-minded friends." With his jackknife he scraped the sides of the gigs until they glistened in the lamplight. He sharpened the points of the hooks on an emery stone and tied the gigs onto heavy hand lines that were wound on boards. He proudly surveyed his handiwork and said, "If I were a cod, I'd sure snap at those."

"Are they just as good as the real boughten kind?" Cookie asked.

"Maybe better. You see, the commercial ones are fish-shaped lead gigs, all gray. These are two colors, copper and silver. Of course we don't know whether or not fish see colors, experts disagree, but we do know that they notice differences in shades. Get into your coat, Cookie. We're going to try 'em."

He turned to me and said, "Honey, I'm sorry about you having to stay in with Bob. Honestly I am. But the first day the sun is out, I'll take you on a super-duper trip. Now you two take care of yourselves. There's lots of eel grass in the water right out here in front of the cabin and you can watch us through the window." Bob's eyes brimmed over and he begged to go along. Bill had to unwind him as the little boy clung onto his coat.

Bob was in a sorry state, so I tore yards and yards of dancing dolls with their hands all joined together from a folded newspaper. It was unbearably hot and humid in the cabin, yet if I opened the door, Bob coughed. While we were steaming through the tenth set of dolls, I smelled smoke. Wisps of it were curling up from the oven door. My chicken! I'd forgotten the beast. I streaked across the room and yanked it out of the oven. It was smoldering and the burned skin had flaked off, exposing meat that was saddle brown. Disgusted, I threw it in the sink. Why don't cookbooks warn a person not to melt solder and roast a chicken at the same time?

Unimproved in mood, I read to Bob. He fretted. We

dressed the kittens in newspaper skirts. He still fretted. In desperation, I dragged a chair to the window so he and I could watch the fishermen. The rain was coming down in sheets, smacking on the tar-paper roof, and the dreary monotony of it nearly drove me crazy. I thought of the play, *Rain*, by Somerset Maugham, and now I had a deeper sympathy for Sadie Thompson; I didn't blame her for anything she did.

Bill and Cookie were in a rowboat anchored about two hundred feet off shore. We watched them toss the giggs into the water, let line slip through their fingers, and then jerk it up several feet. They repeated these intermittent pulls until the line went slack when they hit bottom. Then they gigged the lure up again and repeated the process. It looked deadly dull to me, but they appeared to be having a wonderful time. Through the rain, they resembled figures in the first moving pictures where people moved jerkily and had streaks running from their heads to their toes. Suddenly Bob jumped off my lap and pointed out the window. "Look. Cookie has one." Sure enough, his line was angling out and we heard him yell. Hand over hand, he pulled the line in, but just as the cod surfaced, it zipped out again. But this time it came trotting back. I could see that cod didn't begin to fight like salmon. After the fish had dangled into the boat, there was much handshaking and head waggling as father and son congratulated each other.

It was four o'clock before the two wet fishermen clumped in, leaving little lakes on the floor behind them. Cookie held up three most repulsive-looking fish. They had bulging eyes, reddish-brown skins, and wicked spiny fins up their backs. The points of the tail assembly were sharp as a devil's pitchfork. And they had awful figures, unshapely and lumpy.

"Look, Mother, I got the biggest. And did he fight!" I backed away, uninterested in rock cod. Bill took off his slicker and, as he hung it near the stove, he caught sight of the cremated chicken. He looked at it and then at me. It was just as well he didn't say anything, for my nerves were as taunt as a leader wire with a forty-pound king on the hook. Without a word, he picked up the bird in one hand, the clam shovels in the other, and went outside, humming a funeral dirge.

When he returned, he silently started to skin the cod with pliers. After the liver-spotted skin was off, he sliced the flaky white meat from the ribs and backbone. I opened canned macaroni and fixed a salad while he floured the fillets, making the mess men usually do in a kitchen. Then he measured a third of a cup of bacon grease, a third of vinegar, and a last third of cooking oil into a cold frying pan. It was a weird-looking brew.

"Ben White told me how to do this. He got the recipe from a colored cook from Florida. Wait till you eat it! It's fried fish—with a college education." He warned me never to put this mixture into a hot frying pan or it would sizzle and spatter the hot grease. He also said it was important to let it boil for five minutes as this took the sharp edge off the vinegar.

I had fishwifely reservations about how good cod would be, half-fried, half-boiled. It sounded awful, but later, when Bill lifted delicately browned fillets onto the plates, I began to weaken. With the first bite, I was a convert. Surprisingly, the fish didn't taste a bit sour. It was moist inside with a nice crunchy crust. It was delicious and interestingly different.

Soon after dinner the boys went to bed while Bill
monkeyed with his fishing tackle by lamplight. I had a
long evening to reflect upon the charms of a day in the
country, and I decided that women who agonized over
being fishing-*widows* were wacky.

It rained the next day. Wind-driven rain tested each
section of the tar paper and, when it found a crack, it
came spurting in. Bob now was as husky as an Indian
brave but I had a cold. I couldn't go with the others to
Cascade Lake for trout even if I had wanted to. Which
I didn't. So I stayed alone in the twilight cabin and
knew how the Count of Monte Cristo must have suf-
fered in his dungeon.

It continued to rain the day after that and I broke out
with an advanced case of "cabin-fever"—the kind that
makes women bite themselves in the neck. By now I
knew why pioneer women died young. It wasn't the
hardships—it was pure choice. Father and sons fished.
I fried, boiled, baked, and steamed cod. For a real
change, I sautéed trout. The stove had to be kept cherry
red to dry out clothes and, shrouded in steam, we ate
fish. So did the cats and Bonnie. The most exciting
thing that happened all day was when Felina choked a
a little on a fishbone.

The fourth day was only foggy. Bill and the boys
came home late after spending the day in Cappy Bell's
shack. The smell of their clothes revived olfactory
memories of a night on Waldron Island and their vocab-
ularies were startlingly enlarged and certainly more
colorful. Bob looked puzzled and asked, "Mommie,
what's the difference between a sonofabitch halibut and
just a plain one?"

Bill explained it nicely and said, "The barometer is

shooting up. Cappy said it would be clear tomorrow, so
I've arranged a trip just for you, dear." He told me he
had engaged a country girl to ride herd on the boys.

"Where are we going?" I inquired, speaking slowly
for all my reflexes were rusty.

"After bass. Fresh-water bass. It's all lined up with
Bill Dewhirst." He eyed the pup, swooped her up just
a trifle too late, and continued, "We're going to meet
him at nine and he'll take us to an island owned by a
friend of his. There's a lake on it just lousy with bass.
Grand day, eh?"

It was a grand day; everything clicked. The wet-
sponge world steamed in the sunshine. The rosy-
cheeked farm girl arrived on time. She would be pale
by evening but I was callously unconcerned in my relief
at having someone else hog-tie the children for a while.
I only hoped they wouldn't pull the beach apart or get
the tides all out of kilter.

We drove to the little town of Olga through the most
beautiful countrysides. The weather had completely re-
lented. The freshly washed leaves were Kelly green;
the air, sweet and pungent with growing things. It was
a day only June can dream up. The woods smelled so
wonderful that it was enough to lift the spirit right out
of the body. I was glowing with anticipation as I listened to Bill's account of his last bass trip with this
friend.

"It was in August so we used dragonflies for bait.
Caught 'em first with a silk mesh net as they skimmed
near the edge of a marsh. A whole cigar box of them.
They were used alive, of course."

"Ugh. I hate using live bait, Bill. But how could you
take just one dragonfly out of the box? I should think

all the rest of them would fly away when the lid was lifted."

"They would, if it weren't for Bill Dewhirst's million-dollar trick. When he catches a fly, he holds it upside down and stabs it in the chest with a big pin. This takes a lot of the pep out of him; he can still wiggle his wings but he can't fly." My husband smiled reminiscently, adding, "That was a day. Twenty-seven flies and twenty-seven bass."

"Will we use dragonflies today?"

"Hardly. They aren't out yet. Don't know what we'll use. Dewhirst said he'd bring all the tackle. Told me he had a special lure for the big ones. Whatever it is, we'll get bass. And if he says we'll get big ones, then we'll *get* big ones, for Bill Dewhirst is about the slickest fisherman I know."

We parked our car at Olga and the tiny, sea-girt town smiled back at us. It looked like one of those cut-out villages which children assemble. There was a half-pint post office, a few white cottages guarded by bird dogs and white fences and lovely tall trees. A dock ran out to a float which was gently rising and falling as the waves rippled under it.

"There he is. Hi, Bill," my husband called, pointing to an eighteen-foot boat tied up to the float. The man was puttering with a twenty-two-horsepower outboard motor. As we approached, he looked up and waved. I liked his hearty hand shake, his voice, and his casual manner. He had nice eyes, an English accent, and the lithe body of an outdoor man. Bill had told me that some of the islanders were English or of English descent. having migrated from near-by British Columbia. He said they had the wit, the kindness, and the sturdy independence of Maine farmers—only they were happy about it all. I could see why: this was such a gentle, fertile, smiling land that it couldn't provoke cussedness in anyone.

Bill Dewhirst knew just how to make that mean-tempered motor sit up and take notice. After a few grumbles and a whine or two, we shot away from the float. Multicolored diamonds danced away from the prow while the cobalt waves in our wake oiled over each other before frothing into the white V we left behind us.

"Ever been bass fishing?" our friend shouted to me over the roar of the motor. When I shook my head he said, "You've got a real thrill coming. Now, I have a favor to ask of you both. When we get back, please don't tell anyone where we landed the bass. Don't mention the name of the island, for it belongs to a friend of mine and it's private property. Just like your own back yard."

The sun was warm and almost blinding to me who had been holed in for days. The gulls gleefully rode the air currents above us as though they had been created just for their pleasure. A seal popped up to look us over, and two long-necked loons on a log flapped away as we approached. I was sure this would be one of the most wonderful days in my life.

Too soon the prow nosed into the gravel beach of *The Island* and the men dragged the boat on rollers above the high-tide line. They divided the tackle between them, and I assumed the shoe box Bill Dewhirst tucked under his arm contained the lunch he had promised to bring. We had a mile walk ahead of us along a fairy-book trail, and often it was hard to find it as we tore our way through interlacing salal and Oregon grape. There were heavily wooded stretches where we had to push and pull each other over fallen logs. Huge cedars and firs poked holes in the sky above us. No wonder these mammoth trees had such dignity; they had passed through their smart-alec youth two hundred years ago. Underfoot, their needles and cones, shed from time out of mind, made a springy carpet.

When we stopped on top of a hill for a "breather," Bill Dewhirst said apologetically, "Not much of a trail. But the way to any lake where every cast means a bass is never well marked. And I promise you, there are more small-mouthed bass here than there are big-mouthed politicians in the whole country." Grinning, he added, "And they're just as willing to please, too—if you hand 'em a line they like. Let's go. We're almost there."

The lake lay at our feet over the next rise and I drew in my breath sharply. It was as lonely and lovely as lakes come. Perhaps it was four or five city blocks in diameter, a friendly, playmate sort of lake. The trees were reflected so clearly that it wore a wreath around its shore with a second-hand view of clouds floating in the center. We hoisted each other to the top of a tremendous rock that overhung the water.

"Here we are," my husband said. He laid his gear down on the moss and grasped my hand as we both leaned over the edge of the rock and peered down about ten feet to the water below us.

"Watch," he said, quietly. Then I saw shadows moving. "Those are bass," he breathed, excitement tingling through his fingers to mine. Never before had I seen the fish I was going to catch. Slender long shapes glided past, ephemeral as ghosts. Finally Bill Dewhirst broke the spell, saying, "Those little ones haven't a worry in

the world, but about a dozen grandfathers better call
the priest. Let's set up our rods." Reels clicked into
place and the ratchets whined as the line was fed through
the guides. I'd never been so thrilled. An afternoon
here was reward enough for the past days. So this was
fishing!

Bill Dewhirst told us to choose a hefty leader. When
we both were rigged up, my husband asked what we
were using for bait.

"In the shoe box over there. Not so nice to use, but
it gets the ones that are old enough to know better.
Make a harness and let the hook swing free under the
belly."

Because of our previous talk about dragonflies, I had
a hazy notion we would use some kind of a June beetle.
It seemed definitely psychopathic to make a harness for
a bug and I knew I'd never get used to a fisherman's
hocus-pocus. Curious and very eager, I was kneeling
beside Bill when he untied the string and took the lid
off the box. One look—and even before I could scream,
a great wave of nausea burst in the middle of my
stomach.

That box was half full of live mice!

I fought against the black fog that was closing in
around me. Even with my eyes tight shut, I could see
those mice skittering around. Then, from miles away,
I heard the men talking, saying something about getting
my head down low.

I watched the men lift eleven beauties—from my van-
tage point across the lake. I heard them yell when a big
one flashed into a snag; I saw another kick up white
water a dozen times before it came in. But even from

this distance, I couldn't look in their direction when they unhooked a fish.

All afternoon I sat there, hunkered down on a log. Elbows on knees and chin in hands, I watched them, as forlorn and unloved as those drab ladies pictured in patent-medicine advertisements who have falling of everything, including spirits. But I was resigned. Some men drink, some gamble, and others chase blondes. Bill fished. But I would never go fishing again.

5

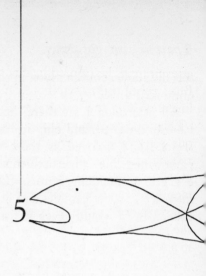

The one that got away

After that week in the country, I was highly allergic to fish—especially on a hook—and Bill knew enough about women never to argue when faced with raised eyebrows and silent hauteur. I'd had the cure and I swore I would never go fishing again, so Bill went alone, with other men or with his sons. I had no misgivings when he brought home a thirty-four-pound king from Orcas nor the numerous messes of silvers from around the Sound. I just started making parsley-butter balls whenever the car stopped in the garage. There was a twinge of interest when he lugged back from Holmes Harbor a handsome set of hooknose silvers he had caught spinning; if the fishing was half

as exciting as he painted it, that trip must have been fun.
But I continued to stay home, nursing my peeve in lone-
liness, well on the way toward being a fishing-widow.

Then one Sunday evening early in September Bill and
our sons came home exuding enthusiasm. They were
radiant and in such fine fettle that I had an uneasy feeling I was missing a lot. They had been up near the
mouth of the Skagit River and brought home a whop-
ping mess of cutthroat trout. With shining-eyed pride,
the boys laid their fish before me and had to be refereed
in a knock-down fight over who had landed the biggest.
They swaggered like true fishermen, not even forgetting
to tell about the big silver that grabbed Bob's line and
cleaned out all his tackle. I knew it would come—the
yarn about the huge one that got away.

My husband, with a sly intuition, didn't speak so much
about the actual fishing as the beauty of the place, the
grandeur of the mountains, and how September's opalescent haze gave a mother-of-pearl sheen to this bit of The
Charmed Land. He told of eating lunch on the hard-
packed beach at low tide and how he had made ten-foot
trumpets for the boys out of kelp by notching it here
and there. So by the time I was rolling these lovely ten-
inch trout in flour, I was feeling a little sorry for myself.

"Mother," Cookie edged his brother away from my
side, "be specially careful with the trout that have the
tails cut off. They're the ones I caught and I don't want
Bob eating *those*. They're mine. See?" A near bloody
battle followed when Bob insisted the biggest tailless
trout was *his*. Hadn't he scooped it up in the net as it
fell off Bill's hook and started to swim away? It was
a moot point so I sent all three males outdoors to settle
it and save wear and tear on the furniture.

I almost hated to gob flour on those beautiful fish, their spots so tastefully arranged on delicately colored scales.

"Why are they called 'cutthroat'?" I called to Bill. He left his role of umpire and came in to show me.

"Don't you see that faint red line under their Andy Gump chins? Looks like a gash and it's brilliant when cutthroats are in fresh water. They're a mighty sporting fish. Go up to ten, fifteen pounds with the right feed and they're sort of a western relative of the Montana black-spotted trout. And you better treat them with respect."

"Why?" I asked. "Are they so hard to catch?"

"No. Plenty of 'em around the rivers' mouths this time of year. They are the three- or four-year-old trout about to go up river to spawn. But, you know, I sort of hate to catch the little guys." He looked at the sizzling panful sadly, adding, "They gave up a lot for me."

"Why this dewy-eyed tenderness?" I inquired.

"Oh, because cutthroat are like steelhead, the only two salt-water fish around here which don't die after spawning. They live to love again. And again. Makes me feel like Elizabeth Barrett Browning's father when I keep young lovers apart and—"

"Very noble," I answered, "and spoken like a man, but tell the boys to come and get them. Hot." While we ate the delicate pink meat, fine-grained and juicy, I secretly was wavering in my determination never to go fishing again. The family certainly had had more fun fishing than I'd had with the Sunday Supplement. The boys still were glowing over the adventure and I was ignored by all males—a bitter pill for any woman. The talk was about pop gear and number one spoons and the tremendous dogfish that followed Bob's hooked trout and nearly got him. They banded together like members at a Rotary luncheon, treating me with the indifference I honestly deserved. So, knowing fishermen would rather bed down with a saber-toothed tiger than a poor sport, I resolved to go fishing on the very next trip.

Ironically enough, fishing was poor and business was good all autumn, and Bill didn't go wandering from the hearth until after Christmas. Of all times, he picked January for his next trip. He spoke of it at dinner one night, quite casually, just as though it wasn't the craziest idea in the world. Or maybe it only hit me wrong, for I had had a hectic day cleaning closets and sorting out junk so that new Christmas presents could be wedged in. This had to be done with no fanfare, for Bill hates to part with anything—he's the kind of person who still has the Valentines he received in the third grade, not to mention his outgrown intern suits and his high school chemistry notebooks. He particularly cherishes each item of clothing in his fishing locker and, just two jumps ahead of the moths, I'd thrown some of the stuff out.

During dessert he looked at me oddly and I was afraid my guilt showed. But he said, "Otto was in the office today and he brought me a pail of fresh steelhead eggs. I'm going up the Skagit River after 'em tomorrow. Want to go along?"

I automatically started to say "No," for I like the marrow in my bones in its native state and not frozen, but I remembered my promise to myself and lied in my teeth. "I'd love to go," I said brightly, and was rewarded with such delighted, husbandly approval, it put me to shame.

After dinner, while Bill fussed with tackle, I laid out four suits of long underwear, two apiece, a two-foot pile of sweaters, and all the wool socks in the house. Sheepskin coats were stacked in the front hall beside the lunch and gear. At last all was in readiness and we went up to bed. Bill set the alarm clock—for four-thirty!

I didn't hear the alarm. Even the light in our bedroom did not wake me. But I stirred groggily when Bill shouted from the basement, "Where in hell is my fishing hat?" A moment later he was in the room, handing me a cup of coffee and demanding to know where I'd put his hat, his bellow only slightly louder than that of a wounded bull. The coffee melted my heart, but bed never had felt so good and I tried snuggling deeper under the blankets.

"None of that. Up and at 'em," he was saying. Then he looked at me squarely and asked, "Where *is* that hat?"

The dreaded question. I knew where the thing was all right—in the bottom of the Salvation Army barrel—and, having no desire to raise our sons on alimony, I dressed quickly and recovered it. The tattered dirty fedora was reminiscent of fish. There were deep sweat stains discoloring the ribbon where a couple of bucktail Royal Coachmen still clung, and the brim was chewed ragged in places, probably the work of pack rats on some camping trip.

"Here it is," I said meekly, and held it out between thumb and forefinger.

"Thanks," he said ungraciously. "Now please lay off this hat in the future. Understand? It packs more luck than a dozen rabbits' feet." Chastened, I whipped out a ten-thousand-calorie breakfast and we started off in the dark. It was going to be a cold fifty miles.

Bill settled down for the drive and breathed the word "Steelhead" reverently. "You know," he said, "there're only two kinds of fishermen in this part of the country—those who have caught steelhead and the poor devils who haven't. Kings and silvers are fine, but they have to have their minds a long way from family life to be as peppy as a steelhead always is. They're plain mean and it's lots harder landing them in a river full of snags than in an acre of salt water. Soon as they're hooked, they head for snags like our kids for watermelon. Of course, you don't know anything about steelhead—"

"I certainly do," I cut in. "I know how to fix them with lemon butter."

"Well, you can forget the fixin's. No lemon around their tails. That is, if we see any tails. There are lots of good fishermen who've never even had a strike."

"What's so tough about them?"

"Steelhead are tricky. You hardly know when you get a bite. They sort of sneak up on the bait, look at the eggs, and think it over and toy with them awhile, you know, like you do with caviar. Sometimes they bump it with their noses and follow it downstream quite a ways before gently taking the bait in their mouths. Now, if you set the hook too soon, when you feel one fooling with it, of course it is snatched away when he is just getting interested."

"What happens if you play safe and wait?"

"That's just as bad. Then he's had time to take it in his mouth, roll it around, and feel the prick of the hook and spit it out again. Remember, steelhead are finicky eaters."

"They sound like sissies to me."

"You'll find out—I hope."

We had turned off the highway onto the road which roughly follows the Skagit River when the brassy sun deigned to rise. Dawn was a steel-blue rim on the horizon and soon we could see the river. Bill, like a fire horse smelling smoke, was stepping on the gas.

"Are we fishing from the bank?" I asked.

"We may have to, but I hope we fish from the boat Otto promised to have hidden where I fished with him before. I think it's easier than casting from the bank, and you can change positions better." He frowned and added, "I told you Otto is a patient of mine and a swell guy but a pretty fancy single-handed drinker. If he went out on a bender last night, I'll bet he forgot the boat. We'll soon see."

A little further upstream Bill pulled off the road and parked the car under some huge fir trees. He tore to the river's edge, peered at it, and returned smiling, delighted to find the water fairly clear and not murky which, he explained, kept the trout from seeing the bait. I was more than delighted to find the day clear, for even halfhearted, watery winter sunshine cuts the cold. While Bill was unloading gear, I stood on the bank and gazed down at the mighty, swift-flowing Skagit.

Everybody's love for this river is tinged with the awe the Indians felt toward it, for its ripping, rushing currents have claimed many lives. We were on an open, sketchily wooded section where the river flowed smoothly, but several hundred yards downstream the water greened and churned white as it swept over a riffle, only to calm down again for another deceptively quiet run. Then and there I decided that any fish that could swim against that current was red-hot stuff, no matter how he ate.

"Good old Otto," Bill called to me. "Here's the boat. Come help me launch it." I dragged and pulled, not sharing his enthusiasm, for I was scared silly of that river. A back eddy snapped the prow around as I got in, and I thought it was like spitting in the eye of Providence to go out at all. Bill waded knee-deep to shove off, and when he climbed aboard, the boat listed heavily. Still unbalanced, we shot downstream before we could trim ship.

"Be careful!" I cautioned, squeezing the words through the tight band around my throat. "If you fell in with those boots on, you'd never have a chance."

He pooh-poohed my fears, let the boat drift to the edge of the current where it by-passed a quiet pool, and dropped anchor. Unconcerned over the river that swirled around us and hissed at the anchor rope, he picked up my two-piece, seven-foot casting rod with its free-running reel.

"Now, if any of the girls in your bridge club ask you about it, tell them you used a number two hand-forged steelhead hook on an eighteen-inch leader, fifteen-pound test. Be sure to explain how this lead-wire sinker is tied onto a short, lightweight dropper string which is tied to the twenty-pound test line where the leader joins it. See?"

He told me the lead sinker would sink to the bottom and, pushed by the current, would dribble along over the gravel while the leader with its baited hook could swing out freely some five or six inches above.

"Remember, my dear, you're not after salmon which plow right into the bait and set the hook by the force of their strike against the spring of the pole. Now steelhead are mean scrappers, but, as I told you, they bite easy. Please hand me that pail of eggs. Be careful with it. Spill that roe and the day's all over."

He pawed around in the bucket and lifted out a long, repulsive chunk of stuff that looked like a colored picture of a lung. A myriad of pale orange-red eggs were held together in this string by tiny grayish membranes. He cut off a chunk about the size of a robin's egg and wove it on the hook, being careful to cover both barb and shank. Then he took a spool of red thread from his pocket and broke off a piece about six inches in length.

"Otto gave me a swell idea," he said, "one of those tips that can mean the difference between catching fish or not. He advised me to bind the eggs on with this matching thread. They stay on the hook a lot better. Some men use a 'strawberry,' but Otto says it scares them off half the time."

"A strawberry, for fish bait?" That sounded crazy to me, and I was sure he had not told me about *all* of his ancestors.

"That's just a fancy name for a wad of these eggs when they are tied into a little gauze bag. It's about the size and color of a small strawberry. But steelhead often nose the bait before they touch it and I've a hunch they can feel the mesh and so lay off."

When both hooks were baited, orange-red and juicy-looking and with the tip of the hook hardly showing at all, Bill stood up in the boat and cast. It was a nice, easy swing and, between wrist and rod action, he plunked the sinker some thirty feet upstream.

"There. That's how. And don't forget to thumb the reel gently while you cast. Just touch it. But thumb it firmly the moment the sinker hits the water. If you don't, you'll get a 'bird's nest' that will be a beauty. And I'm warning you, if you do, you'll be on your own, sweetheart."

He told me how to cast, how to drift the sinker, and said I better just pray about not getting hooked up. I did as he advised, but I didn't have much idea what he was talking about. Anyway, my first cast left the boat— by a good three feet, and my second effort may have gone ten. Then I cast again and began to get the feel of it when the lead plopped into the pool across stream with an exciting little splash. Delighted at my cast, I watched the sinker submerge, completely forgetting to thumb the reel, and the current already had the lead bumping nicely along bottom when I glanced down at my reel. Something awful had happened. Line billowed out all over it, loose loops puffed up while a few tight strands kept the line from going out.

"Look!"

Bill did—and sighed. "That's a 'bird's nest.' Now pull your line in by hand, coil it in the bottom of the boat, and start untangling it. Better slip your leader off, it'll be easier. And, remember, a right thumb is very handy. Bet you don't forget again."

I don't know how long it took me to unsnarl that fouled-up line, but I'd have sworn there was time for a whole generation of steelhead to be born, grow up, and go to sea. I struggled with stiff fingers, for it was decidedly drafty on that river. While I worked and muttered, Bill had a strike and lost it and once he got his sinker hooked up on bottom and had to jerk his line free. But he saved his leader as only the lightweight dropper string broke.

Two fingernails later, my line was snug and smooth on the reel and I cast again. This time, in my eagerness to thumb the reel, I did so before the lead hit the water, which not only broke the length of my cast but also jerked the bait so hard that it pulled apart. It looked as gray and bedraggled as bargain-basement lingerie. I cast repeatedly, improving a little with each try, and decided it was lots of fun. Finally I made a right handsome cast, managed to thumb the reel the split second the lead hit the water, let out line enough to allow the sinker to hit bottom, and was rewarded by feeling that exciting little tremor along the line as the current bounced the lead over the gravel. The boat had pulled anchor a bit and drifted into swifter current, and standing up in that bobbing boat with silver water swirling around us wasn't too comfortable or safe. Woman-like, I chatted to cover my uneasiness.

"Bill, just what is a steelhead? And where do they go after they spawn and leave the river?" Before he answered, he reeled in, replacing the tired-looking gob of eggs that dripped from his hook with a fresh cluster.

"Well," he said absently, his mind on his cast, "authorities generally agree steelhead are sea-run rainbow trout. They resemble them a lot when they are in the river and ready to spawn. Yet when they are at sea they look a good deal like a silver salmon, and I'm told they are the western counterpart of the Atlantic salmon. So you figure it out."

"When do they spawn?"

"In the spring, though the winter run starts going up river in the fall when they are between three and five years old. But they spend most of their lives at sea, and I've a hunch they just hang around the Sound here or the inland waters and feed deep on shrimp spawn. Though for all I know, they may go to California, like the rest of the nabobs. Anyway, they grow big some place, for the world's record rod-caught steelhead tipped the scales at twenty-nine pounds." He looked at my bait as I reeled in, adding, "You need fresh bait."

I sat down, reached for the pail of eggs, put it beside me on the seat, and cut off a gooey mess.

"Hey," he warned, "better take that bait bucket off the seat. Put it down where it's safe and—" He suddenly tensed all over, gave his line a steady, quick little jerk, grinned all over the place, and went to work.

"Got one!" His raw silk glinted in the sunshine as it cut upstream, making a humming sound as it sang through the water.

"Look at that devil get down in her collar and pull." He was shouting at me, leaning forward and nursing every foot of line that ripped off, poised and ready for a lightning cutback. An instant later, the line sagged a bit and he brought it in. With my gear in the boat, I was cheering from the sidelines.

"Watch it, Paw. She's heading for that snag." Just in time, the line grew taut and the tip of the rod arched sharply. With the zest and fervor of a crapshooter, Bill began talking to that trout. "C'mon, sister. Easy there. Let's see you do your stuff." He had checked the run but it was anybody's guess where the fish would head for next.

"Get out in the open and fight fair," he coaxed, gently

tugging that load of dynamite away from the half-submerged log in a pool across stream. I jumped when the fish did. It shot up out of the water gleaming silver against that charcoal black log. The long slender form thrashed its head from side to side trying to throw the hook.

"You can't cough it up, chum," Bill bellowed, "and if you've got any dates, you better break 'em." Then the tip of his rod snapped up and we knew the trout was steaming toward the boat.

"Get out the net," he said, and added, "even though you'll probably have time to knit yourself a pair of socks before we need it." Again the line zinged out as the fish headed for a boulder near the far bank.

"Oh, be careful." I was squealing like a squaw, for I'd lost two sinkers in the water-logged branches behind that same rock. "Look!" I grabbed his arm and pointed to the big limb of a fir tree that was floating downstream. He hopped up on a seat and, just in time, lifted the rod high over his head as the branch swished under the line.

"That was close. For a second there we almost didn't eat fish." He smiled at me approvingly and said, "Thanks, pal, for the warning. I didn't see it." I closed my eyes, savoring the word "Pal." I certainly liked the sound of that, and it came to me all at once that I was having a wonderful time. Why, fishing was fun and—

"Take a look now," Bill crooned softly. During my reverie, the trout had flashed toward the boat and now was lazily finning beside it.

"Want the net?"

"Nope. Try to net her now and you'd find out she still has her fuse lit." That fish must have heard, for she exploded into another run, close to the bottom this time.

"Hold him, Pappy. He's headin' for the barn," I yelled, so excited I didn't realize what I was doing. With the rod pounding in his hands, Bill said, "It'd be a damn sight easier to stand up in this boat if you'd quit jumping up and down." Subdued, my eyes never left that line, for there was a long argument before that steelhead bowed to authority and slowly backtracked toward us, fighting every inch of the way. There was another scrap when she saw the boat, and several short runs before Bill snugged the line up to a rod's length.

"There," he breathed deeply, relieved and exultant. Now we could see it off the prow, dangerously near the anchor rope. It was half on its side, its gills working hard. Gingerly, Bill led him toward the stern and then back and forth the length of the boat several times with the tip of the rod held high, ready for a possible last-minute lunge. He looked at his wrist watch and said, "Twelve minutes. Should be a twelve-pound fish. Pound a minute, the experts say. Hand me the net. Guess it has the wind taken out of its sails."

I knew it was touch-and-go at this point, for, if the trout had any pep left, he'd make a violent jump when he saw the net. Snubbed up this close, there would be a direct pull, enough to snap the leader if it were kinked.

But Bill netted it beautifully, a quick, head-on sweep, and the flailing steelhead was over the gunwale thumping on the floorboards. The hook fell out of its mouth.

"What say?" Bill couldn't resist sticking his thumbs under his armpits. "Isn't a steelhead on the hoof worth two on the platter?" Together we gazed at the beautiful thing at our feet, its sleek two-foot length a blend of silver and pastel shades.

"Boy or girl, Bill?"

"Boy. Its nose is not so stubby as a girl's, but they're both this same gun-metal gray. That's a pretty tasty dish, a steelhead." It still was fighting in the boat, and there was quite a tussle before he could grab it and rap it smartly on the back of the head. Reluctantly, it gave up and lay still, living silver in the sunshine.

"Look at that tail. See how thick and wide it is? That's where he gets his power. It's more muscular in proportion to its size than a salmon's tail. He's trim as a clipper ship." Admiring him, I thought how different he was from those lumpy rock and ling cod with their bulging eyes, uncorseted figures, and liver spots; a steelhead, in dash, temperament, and lines, is strictly Hollywood stuff.

Bill placed his prize in the shade under a seat, covered him tenderly with a wet gunnysack, and baited up again. No strikes. We both covered the river, but there was nothing doing for an hour, which gives a fisherman too much time for introspection. Bill was fidgety. We ate lunch and still no fish, so we reeled in and heaved anchor.

"Going ashore?"

"Nope. Going downstream a bit. Guess the matrimonial agency around here is closed. Hang on tight." The current picked up the boat like a chip of wood and swept us along. Trees flew past us, boulders loomed up beside us, and were lost in an instant and the bank seemed to rush past us. For once I was too scared to talk. Bill was kneeling and using an oar to steer the boat a bit, and I supposed it was safe enough but awfully nerve-wracking.

Then I heard the rush of the shallow riffles. I snapped my head around to see green water churning white as it tore over the gravel bar in the river. When we hit

the small-time rapids, I was as immobile as the steelhead
under the seat. Bill, of course, was actually enjoying
this. He was having a wonderful time. Turning his head
from side to side, he was taking in everything with un-
blinking eyes, and something about his fearless poise
reminded me of a sea gull in command of its swooping
flight. Except that a sea gull doesn't smile. He had
been too busy to notice me, and when I huddled down
in the bottom of the boat he was honestly surprised at
my fears. Then he winked reassuringly and gave out
the physician's by-line, "Say 'Ah.' It'll soon be over."

As suddenly as we had hit those baby rapids, we were
out of them and the boat was coasting in fairly smooth
water, its green grayed with glacial silt.

"This looks like good water," Bill said and dropped
the anchor in a backwash pool. He baited and cast
while I still was fumbling with a cluster of eggs. There
didn't seem to be any joints in my fingers and I had left
all my speedy reflexes back in those rapids. One per-
verse gob of eggs flatly refused to cover the shank of the
hook, the next would not cover the barb, so, exasperated,
I grabbed the pail and set it on the stern seat beside me
where I could see to pick out a better wad of eggs.
Eventually, I wound thread around a good neat job.

"Look, Bill. Isn't that a fine juicy gob?"

"My dear," he said with solemn reproof, "watch your
language. That's not called a 'gob' but a 'goof.' Anyway, you don't seem to like eggs for bait. Next trip
I'll bring flies along. It's lots more sporting but you
don't catch half as many." He pointed to a fast stretch
of water and told me to try that, then settled back, soul-
deep in that mute and philosophic calm indigenous to all
fishermen. And it was wonderful out on that river with

the low-swung winter sunshine splintering through the trees and the water murmuring to us. Bill smiled his approval when I plunked my lead right where he had indicated. I fairly purred.

"This is habit forming—I hope?" He took off his hat and tossed it at my feet, saying, "You'll like it even better when you get a fish. It's your turn now. But put my hat on gently. Don't knock off the pink angel sitting on the brim. Try it."

I did so, not because of its mystic attributes but because the low sun was slanting directly into my eyes. I wondered if it didn't give a "Mrs. Joad" note to the rest of my rag-tag fishing ensemble, for I'm no fancy-pants fisherman. We both peeled off our sheepskin coats. That encounter with the riffles had set our thermostats up.

It was less than ten minutes later when Bill hollered at me, "Wake up! You've got a fish on." Line was clicking off my reel before I knew what had happened and, completely nonplussed, I plunked my thumb on the reel and leaned on it. Hard.

"Darli-n-g," Bill drawled in pain, "give him line. For cripe's sake, give him line. Take your damned thumb off that spool!" The instant the pressure was lifted, the line rolled off.

"Careful. Hold your rod up and keep him away from that log." By now, Bill had reeled his gear in and was at my side.

"Easy does it. No jerks and—look at him jump!"

"That can't be all one fish," I stuttered, reeling hard. If I could help it, he wasn't going to catch me with any slack. Then, for no reason apparent to anyone but another steelhead, that trout began to zigzag upstream across the river until the line looked like a single lacing in a boot.

"Not sure we want him." Bill shook his head and pursed his lips. "He is some kind of a paranoiac. Thinks people are following him and—"

"Whee. Look." My trout was jumping some two hundred feet upstream. It pirouetted into the air, slapped back into the water, and headed for the boat. Even though I took in line as fast as I could, it looped on the water and I was sure I had lost him. Then, not two feet behind the boat, there was a water spout with that trout in the middle of it, throwing his head and lashing his tail. His leap gave me time to get a taut line on him and when he smacked back into the pool, he pulled the tip of the rod down with him to the water's surface. He lit out to starboard with the rod just clearing the gunwale and sideswiped the bait pail off the seat and into the river.

Bill let out a choked cry as he plunged his arm in after it, missing the swirling pail by inches. He slowly shook the water from his arm and his body stiffened all over—a signal for the approaching storm. But he swallowed twice, only glared at me accusingly, and took his wrath out on those eggs, implying their ancestry was canine and not salmonoid.

"Didn't-I-warn-you-not-to-put-that-bucket—?"

"I know, Bill. It's all my fault and I'm so sorry. But I still have him."

"Him?" he bellowed, getting red around the gills. "It damn well better be a 'her.'" He cleared his throat hard enough to remove his back teeth and spoke thin-lipped, each word snapping like the report of a twenty-two caliber rifle. "If it isn't a 'her' and full of eggs, the fishing for today is all over. And now I'm sure of it; woman's place is in the home."

"You take it, Bill," I begged, thrusting the rod at him, appalled by the full import of the accident.

"No. Do as I say and you can land it. But watch *out!*" He was pointing to a snag on the far side of the river. "Hold your rod up and thumb it gently. Gently, I said. The snug line and the spring in the rod will make *her* slow down and think it over."

I had to land that fish. At the moment, I thought all my future happiness depended upon it. And it *had* to be a female—a fully developed female. To that dual objective I prayed. Sex never reared its ugly head any higher in East Lynne than it did in my thoughts at that moment. I begrudged each inch of line as it pulled off the reel, *gently* halting each run toward danger. This was not fun; the stakes were too high. Finally I worked it close to the boat and I was trembling as I "walked" it back and forth several times. Bill held the net and never said a word. Then he netted it quickly, brought it in, and two pairs of eyes were glued on its nose.

"Man, oh man, it's a female." Bill was gurgling and he looked as though he could kiss that blessed short stubby nose. His knife flashed down the silver belly. The pearly gates of Heaven won't look as good to me as the wealth of coral-red eggs that flopped out. He placed them in the folded back lid of his tackle box and then grinned up at me, "How do you like that hat by now? But you better lead a cautious and conservative life for years to come. You've used up all your luck in one fell swoop. Let's bait up."

I had forgotten the hat was on my head and now I

reached up and touched it with loving, fishy fingers. It did seem to have done me a good turn.

"Tell you what, Bill," I said thoughtfully. "Generally I don't believe in charms, but it is very evident that this hat has something—something I need. So let's put it in the center of the boat and fish for it. Winner's keepers. Next one to kill a fish gets the hat. Right?"

"Fair enough. What do you say we have a cup of hot coffee and rest a bit? Hand me your leader. I'll put on heavier lead and we'll 'plunk' while we take time out."

It was lovely on the river, almost warm, and the fragrance of coffee mingling with the crispy pungence of evergreens and that clean, clean smell of the river was wonderful. I watched Bill cast both lines, floppy with a heavy sinker toward the foot of a riffle where he said fish would be on the move. He then laid the rods in the boat and put a foot on the butt of each rod, saying, "This is a long shot. Don't think we'll even get a nibble, and even if we did, we probably can't grab the fish. These babies need your whole attention and anyway, the river isn't rising." He washed his hands over the side before picking up his cup of coffee, but at that I knew he smelled fish on the hand which held his cup, for icy water has no power over fish eggs.

While we drank, he explained that there are three types of steelhead fishing: bait casting, wet or dry fly casting, and plunking which is still-fishing. He told me why steelheading is so popular in the Pacific Northwest, not only because the trout are such fierce battlers but also because this fishing comes in the winter and early spring when other fresh-water fishing either is closed or dormant. He went on to say that if we were really serious-minded anglers, we would neither use a net nor even a gaff hook, but would play the fish until we could lift it out of the water by the gill covers.

I was tired and I rubbed my back, telling Bill that casting took the snap out of all thirty-two vertebrae. He agreed happily, took a mighty gulp of coffee, and said the sportsman's life never is easy.

"Except Ted Sternholm's." He chuckled and settled back comfortably. "Ever tell you about him? Ted's quite a guy, lives on one of the smaller San Juan Islands, and he's a crack shot. Best I ever knew. Every fall he brings in the biggest deer and brings it in first. He's the kind of a shot who eats pigeon pie with a side order of quail and has pheasant for dessert." Bill looked over the lines and sighed with deep satisfaction before continuing. "Ted's dead-eye Dick all right, but the odd part about it is that he's the laziest fellow alive. Hates to move. He'd rather let a mosquito sting him than bother to brush it off. He drawls his words, drags his feet, and spends most of his life in the rocking chair in front of his cabin.

"I wondered how he ever got up enough steam to be such a crack shot so I asked another Islander about it. 'Tell you, Bill,' he said, 'I figger it this-a-way. Ted's terrible lazy and that's for sure, but by the time he gits where the game is, sights it, and draws a bead on it, he's bound to shoot it. Ain't got energy left to wiggle.' "

As he finished the story, Bill was bringing in lines. We thumbed our noses at plunking and baited up with firm fresh roe. It behaved well and Bill's lure had a sly nudge almost at once. But he didn't get it. Then I felt something bump my line and I set the hook. Still no results. For such big lusty fish, steelhead surely were finicky eaters. By now I had begun to get the hang of casting, the wrist action and the swing and the nice little snap it gives to the lure. Contented, we fished quietly for a while, stealing sidelong glances at the old felt hat which lay between us.

"Why do steelhead live after spawning when salmon die?"

"I don't know," Bill answered, "unless it's because they're a trout and not a salmon. Anyway, this time of year it's safe to get steelhead upstream a bit; they're still good eating. Which reminds me that salmon ready to spawn are something you'd never forget. At that time a salmon looks alive but tastes dead. I learned that years ago when George and I went fishing. We were the greenest of greenhorns."

I settled back for another fish story. Bill cast and then continued, "Neither of us ever had caught a king salmon. We didn't know a thing about them or any salmon, for that matter. We were staying at the inn at Lake Quinault and somebody loaned us gear so we high-tailed it up a tiny little stream. I don't know what we expected to get in August, but anyway we went, hell-bent for fish. The country was so beautiful we hiked miles along that stream and, by the time our feet hurt, the rivulet was hardly wider than a drainage ditch. We sat on a mossy bank and dropped our lines in, good stout ones with hooks no trout would look at. Nothing happened until George was nearly pulled into the stream; he began shouting and swearing and jumping all at once. We could see it, that huge fish that darned near filled up the brook, and it just sort of flopped around. We figured it didn't fight much because there wasn't enough water to fight in—like a whale in a swimming pool. It almost came in when George whistled, and he could have led it out with a leash.

"Finally he got disgusted, waded in, and pulled it out by the gills. We later found out it weighed forty pounds, but as it lay at our feet, it was a sorry-looking thing, dirty gray and bronze, with whole chunks taken out of it, and if I'd had it for a patient, I would have diagnosed its skin condition as eczema. Its tail was half gone. It looked terrible.

"But George was tickled silly. Here was a mighty king, even though he wasn't the fighting giant we'd heard about, and we thought it had just been battered in the landing. As George took the hook out of its mouth, he shook his head sadly and said fishermen certainly were liars, for he'd always heard you strained a ligament landing one that big. And why worry about a missing tail when there was some thirty-nine-and-a-half pounds left?

"He was proud as punch, had his picture taken with it, and we took turns packing it out. When we got back to the inn, we threw it in the car and started for home immediately, planning the big dinner party he'd have the next night.

"When I arrived the following evening, the others already were there, and as we drank our cocktails, I noticed that something smelled awful. It was tough luck to have a dinner party when the drains were stopped up or perhaps the gardener had put fish fertilizer on the lawn that day. I sniffed but couldn't quite place that smell; I'd never run into anything like it. Didn't go too well with the deviled crab canapés. George and his wife were uneasy also.

"After we were seated at the dining table, that king

salmon on a huge silver platter was set before the smiling
host, but he had to work at that smile as he served it. It
smelled fishy all right, but there were undertones and
overtones of something far worse. George and his wife
took the first bites, dropped their forks, and grabbed
their water glasses, swallowing hard. It became a ritual.
We all did the same and, for the rest of the meal, we
toyed with it, hid chunks under our vegetables, and
sneaked bits under pieces of bread. Nobody could eat it.

"Then Jim Bently, a crackerjack fisherman, asked
George where he had caught it. George told him and
Jim bit back a smile as he said innocently that upstream
salmon had a flavor all their own. Anyway, everybody
was polite and nothing more was said about that salmon.
Next day I—

"Whoa there," Bill yelled. His reel flew around and
his line pounded out. "Got one. Give me that hat."

I was reeling in to get out of his way when my rod
arched, tip to the water. This was no time to be hooked
up on bottom, so I jerked the line a little, expecting to
haul out a tangle of waterlogged trash. But instead, my
line sang out and the tip of the rod vibrated, notching
V's against the dark bank, like the jagged graph lines on
a chart.

"Hey!" I shouted. "Don't touch that hat. It may be
mine. I've got one too." A couple on at once, two rip-
snorting steelhead. This was a regular aquarium. Bill
was grinning and grumbling and mumbling words which
were mild and homespun beside Cappy Bell's go-getters,
but they still packed a wallop.

"Listen," he said, handling that rod so beautifully that
it seemed an extension of his arm, "you have to talk to

steelhead. Soothe 'em. They're flighty as coloratura sopranos."

"Quit your fussin' and feudin', Fanny, and come on in," I hollered at mine, hoping Bill's suggestion would keep it away from that half-submerged log.

"Not like that," Bill said, disgusted. "Told you they're prima donnas. Use standard English with a Back Bay accent if you can swing it. You are talking to the aristocracy, remember." He was reeling in fast, for his trout had decided to high-tail it downstream after mine, and our lines cut into the water only fifty feet apart. Bill was worried.

"If those two gals ever get together and talk their troubles over, we are sunk. If they wrap their lines around each other—" Just in time, he pulled a master stroke, gently thumbed his reel, lifted the rod high so the fish got the full spring of it, and halted the run. There was enough authority to stop it, yet not enough to drag the hook out of its mouth. Rebelling at her stage manager, that prima donna had hysterics, jumped up, and threw her weight around.

"Wish I could slip her a little barbital," he muttered. But I was only half listening. I had troubles of my own, for my trout was making wild circles in that pool and I was having difficulty trying to keep a tight line on it and, if the trailing sinker ever tangled into a sunken branch, the sudden jerk might dislodge the hook. I needed the breaks so, rod held high, I stooped down and reached toward the fishing hat.

"No you don't," Bill was grinning, but he shook his head. "No cheating. Play fair and lay off that hat or I'll tell your grandchildren on you. Don't—" His words ended in a grunt as his steelhead zinged up river and now, back to back, we were fighting our trout. I heard him yell when it jumped; I heard it splash back into the stream. Then I heard Bill swear with a heavy business-like rhythm that had a chill of finality about it and I snatched a quick glance over my shoulder. When I saw his face I knew there was only one fish on now.

"Weak leader," he snorted.

"Or a strong back?" I taunted, maliciously. With scant Christian sympathy for his plight, I worked my steelhead out of that pool more by good luck than remote control, until it was beside us, half drifting, half swimming in the shadow of the boat. I had forgotten my grandmother's dire warning that "Pride goeth before a fall" and I was in high spirits—higher than the tip of my rod.

Then it happened—a leap, a showering splash, and a mighty jerk. The empty leader flew up in the air with just a shred of steelhead on the hook.

"She's gone," I wailed, still befuddled and hardly believing it. I gaped at Bill open-mouthed, and just for a second he reminded me of a rooster with its neck outstretched and its feathers ruffled, ready to crow. Then he got hold of himself and said, "Tough luck. You played it beautifully. It's still been a swell day. One apiece. Not bad, though we'd be within the law if we each had four more. They'll have to tighten up on that limit soon or there won't be any steelhead left. Well, let's get going."

Still too disappointed to talk, I sought comfort from the one fish I had landed; I pulled the gunnysack off and admired its shimmering length. At last I said, "Bill, when my friends ask me how much it weighs, what'll I tell them?"

"I don't know what you'll tell them," he answered, "but it weighs about ten pounds."

The sun was settling down in the tips of the fir trees and our sheepskin coats felt good. Bill picked up his fishing hat and put it on, saying, "It's cold and I'm going to wear this now. But I'll be perfectly honest about it. The bet's still on. We'll hold this hat in escrow and fish for it again. Want to?"

"Just tell me when," I answered.

The king is dead

One evening several years and several dozen fishing trips after that first steelhead bonanza, I was waiting anxiously for Bill to come home to dinner. I had big news. Finally I heard him drive into the garage and I listened carefully, wondering how he would close the car door. He generally shut it softly, which meant everything was normal and routine, but a slam foretold a different story; either he was worried or on top of the world. Tonight he slammed it.

It wasn't worry, for he bounced into the room, yelled for the children, and tossed his hat across the living room. The boys nearly knocked him over in their excitement, for they had a hunch such enthusiasm meant family fun.

"Guess what?" he said. "Mac McKenzie was in the office today and invited us to go on a cruise next week. That *Mac-Beth* of his is a honey, a forty-five footer and—"

"Kids too?" Bob cut in, tremulously.

"Sure. The whole family. Their children are going along. Think of it! We're to spend a whole week in the San Juan Islands, in June when the king salmon are in." Shouts prevented further talk; two hilariously happy boys of eight and ten can make almost as much noise as a Republican convention.

Dinner was only half chewed for we all talked at once, and it was almost over before things simmered down enough for me to spring my news. It was a bit touchy so I had laid my plans carefully.

"Darling," I said to Bill, "my great-grandfather and great-grandmother, David and Hannah Forbes, are arriving next week from New York."

"Good Lord." Bill dropped his fork and stared at me. "Didn't know you had any. Have you got relatives behind every bush? How long they going to stay?"

"Forever."

"Are they on stretchers?"

"No. On canvas." I'd had my fun so I hastened to relieve that strained look he had about the gills.

"It's like this. I received a letter today from a distant cousin I didn't know I had, telling me the old family home in New York City is being closed up and she asked me if I wanted the portraits of David and Hannah. Unframed and C.O.D.," I added uneasily. But my strategy had worked; he never blinked an eye. He was so delighted that they were not arriving in the flesh, he welcomed them in oil. He obviously didn't know the price of gold-leaf frames, and I felt this was no time to enlighten him.

"Sure we want them," he said, jovially. "Even C.O.D. If they are any good, we'll enjoy 'em. If not, Hannah may be useful. If she's an acid-looking old biddy, I'll hold her up to you as an example of what you may become if you don't quit pestering me to go fishing." He smiled at me fondly, adding, "Next week you may get your first big king."

There was not much time to wonder about the ancestors during the next few days as I was busy planning for the trip. Both cool and warm clothes had to be sorted out for all of us, tennis shoes dug up, and our dog and cat farmed out to my sister, Virginia. Beth McKenzie and I held lengthy telephone conversations about who would provide what in the line of food. Bill and the boys, tingling with anticipation, checked over the fishing tackle, and one night my husband came home with a huge nautical chart of the San Juan Islands—all one hundred and seventy-two of them.

After dinner we stretched it flat on the dining room table and pored over it, charting many possible courses. There was Orcas Island, like a great horseshoe in this land-locked sea, triangular-shaped Waldron Island, and deep-bayed Lopez. Fathom numerals showed the depths of the channels which swirled and churned between the islands. There were over one hundred fathoms in President's Channel but only six in Pole Pass. With a pencil, Bill pointed to the dotted area hugging almost all shore lines. This was shallow shoal water well under ten fathoms where eel grass grew. He explained how herring attached their white, pinhead-sized spawn to this long slender grass. And salmon follow herring.

We could see why those famous salmon banks off the San Juan Islands were so turbulent; they took the brunt of all the sweep and force of Juan de Fuca strait. Cookie traced the zigzag international boundary line running between the San Juan Islands belonging to the United States, and the Gulf or Channel Islands which are under the Canadian flag. The boys asked us how such an ir-regular line had been determined and we promised to find out on the trip.

On the chart, we could see why fishing is apt to be best off points of land which jut out into the water. Points have wider shoal waters where wind and tide have deposited more sand and, too, tides run more swiftly around points. This means more herring are brought in from deeper water, which partially explains why salmon like active, moving currents. Bill indicated the shoals off Peapod rocks near Point Lawrence on Orcas Island and said they were Cappy Bell's favorite—and almost private—halibut banks. Here was the deep water and sandy bottom which halibut prefer. With Bob's finger he traced the outline of Fossil Bay on Sucia Island and said each boy would find plenty of fossils there. At this point Bill jumped up and ran down to the basement, returning with a small spade and chisel which he added to the "Lest we forget" pile accumulating in a corner of the dining room. Back to the chart, he pointed to the western shoreline of Orcas Island and showed us where he had camped every summer he had been in college. Dropping his finger south an inch, he said, "This is West Beach. Years ago, it used to be dotted black with Indian canoes, for it's one of the hot-test fishing grounds in the islands. Cedar-bark nets were run just inside this tiny point and there were acres of clams and a wonderful spring near by. Clams, salmon, water, and a wide shallow beach. That's why they held their powwows there."

The boys' eyes were round and wide when he told about a doctor who had homesteaded part of lovely little Macia Island long ago and how he had died there alone because he had neglected to arrange for smoke signals which the residents on Orcas could have seen. He said we'd see the moss-covered remains of his cabin and we'd visit Captain Harnden and his family, who were the only people living on Sucia Island. There were stories about Stuart Island and the Spencers who owned Blakely Island. Bedtime came all too soon.

We were scheduled to leave on Thursday, and all day Wednesday I kept adding stuff to the growing pile in the dining room. Bill topped it off with two new red life jackets for the boys—and his fishing hat. That night both lads slept restlessly and called out several times. I mistakenly put this down to their mounting excitement.

In the morning, they were fussy so I shooed them out of the house so I could pack in peace, and I would have done so only, of all times, Hannah and David arrived. The express man plunked the big crate down in the center of the living room and, fearfully, I began to pry it open. As each board came loose, I worked faster and faster, my doubts whirling ahead of me. I knew David had been master of a clipper ship and I hoped he wouldn't look like a sailor on Saturday night. And Hannah. Would she have the long family nose, which, come to think of it, bore close resemblance to the beak of a sea gull? They hadn't better! The C.O.D. had been ten dollars and thirty-four cents. When the last

board came off, I grabbed the excelsior-padded can-
vases, tossed the shredded stuff aside, and stood them
against the wall. Backing away, I took a deep breath and
looked at them.

They were beautiful!

Two exquisite portraits gazed back at me, cool and
serene amid the litter of packings. They might have
been done by an itinerant artist but he had been a fine
one. A hundred years had crackled the paint a little but
only mellowed the colors, and the skin tones were clear
and life-like. First I studied David. His brown eyes almost twinkled at me. Perhaps he had tipped the artist!
Nice half-smiling mouth, and I'd certainly point out to
Bill that his long slender hand holding a book was most
aristocratic. I warmed to his "live-and-let-live" face; it
was going to be easy to get along with David.

But Hannah was different. I sensed that immediately,
for she was the speaking image of my own grandmother,
Julia, her daughter. Julia, who had lived with us when
I was a child, had been beautiful in a Dresden-doll sort
of way. But I well remembered how her tininess had
been deceptive, a Victorian miniature who packed an
Elizabethan punch. As Hannah sat there in her white-
collared, black taffeta dress, I was fascinated by the like-
ness. Those same cool, gray appraising eyes! Mother
and daughter were alike. Both their mouths would have
been pretty if not so primly tucked in at the corners.
Hannah was handsome all right, but in that patient, for-
bidding way fashionable with virtuous wives of the period. Even her neighbors must have called her "a sound
and moderate woman."

Then Hannah practically spoke to me! I was thinking about the kind of frames I'd buy. Real gold leaf

would cost the same as the new outboard motor we needed, and I had about decided to compromise on cheaper metal-leaf imitations when I caught Hannah's eye. She was reminding me of what my grandmother had so often told me with a sniff: "Beware of tarnished finery."

That did it. As I mentally began to juggle my budget, it dawned on me that she would continue to pass judgment on everything I thought and did, would become, in effect, my painted conscience on the wall. Even though the portraits were interesting as a pair, I toyed with the idea of sticking great-grandmother out of sight and living happily in sin with her tolerant husband. But I knew Hannah would never stand for that.

Finally I tore myself away from the pictures and went on with my packing, laying out several books on fishing. I was boning up on the love-life of the salmon, for thereby hangs his downfall.

We were to board the *Mac-Beth* at two o'clock, and around one, Bill came tearing in, his pockets all lumpy with jars of three-inch herring and boxes of plugs.

"Look at this new plug," he said happily, thrusting it under my nose. "It's a red-head. Ought to lure males at least and—"

"Red-heads don't interest brunettes," I answered coldly. "They're unreliable and temperamental and anyway, most authorities think fish don't see colors. Plugs are painted to attract buyers, not fish. Come see Hannah and—" I didn't finish because the boys, whom I had sent upstairs for a last hot bath, came zooming into the room. Dripping wet, they stood there, stark naked. Bob whimpered as his brother disgustedly pointed to him and shrieked, "Look, Daddy."

We did—and our spirits touched bottom. On Bob's stomach and young Bill's back where he couldn't see them were a dozen or so king-sized pimples, big watery ones. Bill grabbed the children, examined them with care, and then said slowly, "Chicken pox." Dragging his feet, he went to the telephone, called the McKenzies, and asked if they and their children had had chicken pox. All of us were hanging on his expression. He listened, then his face lit up like a Wurlitzer and he fairly sang out, "So long. We'll be seeing you." He slammed down the receiver and threw an arm about each son. They still were stricken, afraid they were to be left home. But the despair in their eyes turned to delight when their father chucked each boy under his chin and said, "It's okay, fellas. All the McKenzies have had it. You're going, though you may have to be quiet a day or so. What's a few pimples between fish? Now scoot and get dressed." The walls reverberated with their shouts but I didn't feel so happy about it. Then Bill patted my shoulder reassuringly, saying "There's nothing better than salt air—and calamine lotion—for chicken pox. They'll be all right. Let's get going."

This near-tragedy knocked Hannah and David out of my mind, and I forgot about them until everything was packed in the car and the family was yelling for me to come. But I had to take a wifely last-minute look about the house, and as I checked doors and windows, I avoided Hannah's eyes, knowing she would disapprove of our casualness over illness. She might have wished a pox on me, too.

Beth and Mac McKenzie already were aboard when we arrived at the Yacht Club dock. Their tow-headed, freckled Dick dashed down the slip to meet us. He was an engaging child, about the same age as Cookie, but as blonde as our sons were dark. His younger sister, Barbara, shyly hung behind him. Big, sandy-haired Mac boomed his welcome and Beth smiled at us over a case of canned milk. Before we set foot on deck, Bill tied the bright red life preservers on Cookie and Bob and made them promise never to take them off while on the cruiser.

Stowing eight people, most of the food for a week, and all of our paraphernalia aboard a forty-five foot boat needed sardine packer's technique. Bed linen, dry groceries, and tinned food were jammed into the lockers under the bunks, perishables in the tiny ice box, and fishing gear in the toilet. Rods were laid on the cabin roof. Everything was shipshape before we cast off and started across Portage Bay.

It was a crystal June day and the Gothic buildings of the University of Washington stood out like fine etchings. Both the Cascade and Olympic Mountain ranges were standing guard over this evergreen land and even imperial Mount Rainier deigned to come out of her mantle of clouds. We proceeded under the high University bridge, across Lake Union, and into the man-made channel which leads to the locks. Mac cut speed as we approached the first huge gate. It was closed so he idled the engine while we waited with several other small craft.

"Mommie, are we really going downstairs in a boat?" Bob asked. Beth explained to the children that the lakes in Seattle are some twenty feet above sea level and that we had to go through the locks, second largest in the country, to drop the twenty feet to the Sound. Our boys were agog when the ponderous gates opened in the center and slowly swung toward us. Four boats which

had just come in from Puget Sound pulled out of the
chamber we were about to enter. Carefully we and our
companion ships edged into the enclosure, our rope
bumpers dangling overside in case we rubbed against
another boat or the green slime-covered cement walls of
the great chamber. When all of us were crowded in,
lines were passed from each boat to attendants, and made
fast, so the cruisers would not jostle about too much
when the water dropped in the chamber. It dropped
fast. All the skippers and crews were busy, holding the
boats away from each other and the wall which grew
higher as the water rushed out of the lock. But the men
on board each boat stopped their bantering as the water
ceased running out and the attendants threw lines down
to the cruisers over twenty feet below them. There was
a scramble to gather in line before it tangled in propellers. Then, ahead of us, the gates to adventure and the
San Juans swung open and we nosed through into the
sparkling blue of Puget Sound.

That night we dropped anchor in Port Madison at the
northern tip of Bainbridge Island. Before we turned in,
Mac said we would have to leave by six the next morning so as to arrive at treacherous Deception Pass by
slack-tide, the only time when it was perfectly safe to
go through.

After a restless night's sleep on my hard "shelf," I
helped the skipper get breakfast en route. Bill took the
wheel while Mac presided at the griddle; his pancakes
were a specialty of the house and it was a man-sized job
to keep that crowd all eating at once. Whatever else
chicken pox might be doing to our sons, it wasn't im-
pairing their appetites.

During our early lunch, Mac didn't say much. He

looked worried. At ten knots an hour, he had estimated our arrival at the Pass by noon when the tide would be slack, neither ebbing nor flowing. But he had bucked a heavy tide and headwind part of the way and we were going to be late at the Pass for the slack water. It was almost twelve-thirty when we rounded Hoypus Point and saw the Pass ahead of us between Fidalgo and Whidby Islands.

"We can just make it," Mac said seriously. "The tide doesn't run fast the first half hour, but only a powerful boat—or a damn fool—would venture through later when the tide gets going."

At reduced speed we started through this narrow cut between the islands, and the sea rushed and swirled like a river on a rampage. It was only about two hundred yards across, yet unimaginable volumes of water funnel through with each tide. The water boiled; the boat staggered a little and I tightened the life jackets on all four children. Looking down we saw huge whirlpools a foot deep suck at the boat and try to drag us toward the rocks just under the surface. The whole cruiser vibrated as the engine labored, and the noise from our exhaust bounced back loudly from the rock walls of the Pass. I was plain scared but the men were just intent. Slowly, Mac skirted the foaming eddies and we emerged into a little bay that led into beautiful Rosario Straits.

We dropped anchor in the cove and all took naps before heading north toward Point Lawrence. Later, when we were under way again, Beth and I relaxed in canvas chairs on the after deck. Now there were islands all around us; we cruised past Decatur and between Blakely and Cypress Islands which are some five miles in length and almost as wide. The fir trees on Blakely

marched up its hill so evenly they reminded me of people in a theater as seen from a front seat. The water was
a shimmering, silver-flecked blue and, to the west, great
banks of clouds were congregating to welcome the sunset just a few hours away. Two hundred miles off the
stern was Mount Rainier, still imposing and majestic.
Little waves rolled gently up the crescent beaches which
bite irregularly into the islands. Graceful gray-winged
sea gulls slid down air currents as though they were on
wires. We agreed that life had little more to offer.

Dinner over, Beth and I had just finished washing the
dishes and stacking them in their racks when Bill called
us on deck. We were nearing Point Lawrence.

"That's salmon water," Bill said, nodding toward the
tumbling crisscross waves off the point. "The tide's
about full so we won't be able to gig for herring. You
have to get them when the tide's running strong. Too
bad. But probably we can buy some from Cappy.
Say—" he leaned forward and shaded his eyes with his
hand—"isn't that Cappy out there in the dinghy, rowing?" With binoculars, he was sure of it, and he kept the
glasses trained on the old man while we closed the gap
between us.

I went below to change my cotton clothes for heavy
wool slacks and shirt, regretting I looked so very feminine in so many places. I grabbed our boys long enough
to put them in warm clothes, too, for it gets cold on
the water at night.

When I heard Bill yelling, I ran out on deck. Mac
had idled the engine and just off our prow was Cappy
in a tiny eight-foot dinghy. His face was a sunset rose
which meant he was seven sheets to starboard, and he

was pulling on the oars hard, rowing with all his strength toward shore.

"Hi, Cappy," Bill was shouting through his hands, "Going to a fire?"

"Nope. Gonna make one for this here halibut." He glanced at us and grinned as he spoke, but he didn't miss a stroke and now he doubled far forward, thrusting the oars back for a long sweep. Just then a broad flat tail flapped up from the floor boards of the dinghy and smacked Cappy Bell right in the face. We all howled with laughter at once. Evidently he was beyond feeling pain, but he jerked his head back angrily and spewed out some words which should have quieted anything. We could see the halibut; it was half as long as the dinghy and almost as wide. A few strokes later, the same thing happened again—the great broad tail slapped Cappy as he bent over the oars. That halibut's timing was perfect. I stopped laughing long enough to ask Bill why he didn't knock it out.

"If you'd ever tried to knock out a halibut, you wouldn't ask. Your ignorance is showing. They just don't knock out easily. Why, I've seen them thump around on the beach even after they were cleaned. Some goofy kind of reflexes, I guess." Bill left us saying he was going ashore in our dinghy to get herring from Cappy.

Mac started the engine and we followed alongside Cappy's boat inshore as far as we dared, enjoying the show. I was fascinated by that huge fish. It was sort of kite-shaped, whitish and flat, and it had both eyes on the upper side of its head. A slap from that tail must have hurt.

Cappy and Bill met at the floating bait box which was

sunk in the center of a raft anchored several hundred feet from the beach. The old fisherman climbed out of his boat all right, but he walked on the log raft as though he were on a rolling deck and his legs weren't long enough. Bill hung onto his belt as he leaned over the open bait box and netted a dozen live herring. Cappy wavered up, teetered on the brink of the bait box, and said, "Thash right, Bill. If you wanna eat fissh, use fissh for bait. Why feed 'em tin when they want herrin'?" Cappy doubled up his fists and added thickly, "My herrin' will lick a dushen plugs. Git goin' now. There ain't a moon so them kings didn't feed lash night and they oughter be hungry. Hope you ain't forgot me in your will if one of them bastards pulls you overboard." With a floppy arm, he whacked Bill on the back, defying gravity as he managed to totter into his boat. Bill put the wash tub with its still live and swimming herring in our dinghy and returned to the cruiser.

Beth and I were grim as we tucked our exhausted children into their bunks. Such a spectacle as they had just seen! That was as close as I meant them to get to Cappy Bell. Bristling, I met Bill on deck and buzz-sawed my opinion of his friend. He and Mac were rigging up their tackle. He only half listened and then spoke off-handedly: "Say, if those kids are around Cappy, he'll teach 'em how to fish. And they'll remember his skill long after they've forgotten him, his habits, and his words. Mac, hand me those pliers."

Still sizzling, I plopped down in a chair and watched the men rig up three rods with "Orcas Island setups." Crescent sinkers with swivels at both ends were tied to the forty-pound-test cuttyhunk line. Then six-foot lengths of number five steel leader wire were twisted into the free swivel on the crescent sinker. At the end of each leader was the ingenious hook arrangement which consisted of a single steelhead hook above two large triple hooks, the single lead hook so wired that it could be moved either up or down the leader to accommodate herring of different lengths. The two triple hooks were about four inches apart on the leader and had several strands of wire running between them for extra strength.

"Now," Bill explained to me, "the trick is to get herring on these setups just like Ira Yeager does. He showed me how. The herring should just slowly revolve in the water at the right trolling speed. You have to fool a king into thinking that this bait is a wounded herring." He stuck the lead steelhead hook up through the jaws of a live, squirming herring. I gulped but gritted my teeth and watched him jab one prong of the top triple hook into one side of the wriggling fish. Then he did the same thing with the lower triple hook on the other side of the herring, inserting the point fairly near the tail of the eight-inch fish.

"You see," he said, "silver salmon and kings have very different ways of going after herring. Silvers swim fast enough to strike at herring as they go along; they just dart out and grab them. But kings are too slow for that, so they find a school of herring and thrash through it, wounding some of them by the lashing of their powerful tails. Then the wily old devils just wait and snap up the injured stragglers."

Mac started up at trolling speed and Bill threw out the lines separately, testing the action of each herring on its setup. He set the six-ounce slip sinker just a few feet up on the cuttyhunk line to keep the lure under the surface. In turn, he observed the lines critically. The first had that perfect slow roll he wanted but the herring on the others had to be adjusted several times, lead hooks moved a trifle, and triple hooks set differently. He must have spent ten minutes fiddling with them and the whole business looked messy to me. I told him I preferred nice clean plugs or spoons.

"Spoons have one advantage," he said as he adjusted a herring for the fifth time. "When you do get a fish on, he's there to stay. You lose more on plugs but you're apt to get more strikes, too. Sort of evens up." He tossed the setup over the side and peered down at it, satisfied at last with the helpless fluttery movement. Reeling in, he continued, "Near river mouths, when fish are no longer feeding and are irritable as fat ladies on a diet, they are mean enough to strike at any fast-moving object. Then a sweet-acting plug that darts out to either side is good. But around here, salmon are still feeding so nothing beats fresh bait. Well, we'll see. Here are your rods, gals. Let out about fifty feet of line and set your slip sinkers back about twenty feet. I'm going to let out seventy-five feet and try it deeper. And," he looked at us each threateningly, "hold your rods straight out to the side unless you want to get tangled up with my line off the stern. I'm warning you, it would be a hell of a mess."

Lines all set, we trolled across the turbulent point and headed north close to the rock cliff. The water was clean, there was very little seaweed, but occasionally we pulled in our lines to inspect them and perhaps take off tufts of sea lettuce or wisps of eel grass. Behind us on the mainland, Mount Baker was turning from rose to mauve as the twilight deepened. The time was right, because kings, like all sophisticates, dine late, seldom striking before deep dusk. This, I thought, was most considerate of them, for the world is so beautiful at sunset, but I heartily disliked their dawn breakfast hour.

It was cold on deck but the pungent salt air felt good on our faces. I was thinking about Bill and Bob, glad I had discovered no new poxes, when something hit my line and gave it several good jerks.

"Bill. I've got one!" But the ratchet never made a sound and the line was not going out.

"Oh, no, you haven't," Bill said disgustedly. "It's either a dogfish or a cod. Probably a doggie. Reel in quickly and I'll knock it off your line. Damned pests take up a man's valuable fishing time. Horse it in. It won't fight."

It didn't. That dogfish came to the boat with very little struggle, but twisted about wildly as Bill gaffed it. He knocked it out before using pliers to take the hooks from its revolting slit-like mouth on the under side of its body. It was long and thin, gray on its back and sickly white underneath; it had a sort of squat, triangular-shaped body. Its eyes were a true emerald green.

"What is a dogfish, Bill?" Beth asked, stooping down to see it better.

"Oh, it's a member of the shark family and about as worthless as the rest of them. It's primarily a bottom fish—you can tell that by the mouth on the under side—so you're more apt to get 'em if you troll too deep or too slowly. I've heard that during the First World War dogfish were canned for food, after being processed for about a week, I guess. They're tough as seven devils. But that didn't work. There was something in the meat that ate right through the can and—"

"Look!" Beth screamed, pointing to the still quivering

dogfish. She was on her knees, babbling, "What, what—"
I looked, blinked, and was as amazed as she. For a tiny
wiggling dogfish about four inches long had just been
born that minute. Right on deck. It was a perfect little
replica of its mother. Another one was on its way.

"Yes," Bill said, lifting the battered setup from the
fish's mouth. "Dogfish are cold-blooded but live-bear-
ing and should be consigned to hell." Unemotionally,
he scooped up the infants and heaved them over the side,
tossing the mother in on top of them.

"Oh, Bill." Beth was amused at her own concern. She
was so petite and blonde and appealing that the tenderness in her blue eyes was touching.

"They'll make out all right, Beth. Anyway, I didn't
come out here to practice obstetrics. You put my line
out, Bea, while I fix this mangled setup. Time's a-wast-
ing."

Instead, I handed the rod to Mac and relieved him at
the wheel so he could fish. I was tired and the monot-
onous chug, chug of the engine made me even more
sleepy. Yet I had to keep my wits sharp for other cruisers and smaller outboard motorboats which were con-
tantly dodging in front of us. Often it was difficult not
to cross their lines with ours. When there was a clear
stretch ahead, I relaxed and let the prow nose its way
through the sunset-stained, copper water and gazed
dreamily toward distant Sucia Island. I wondered how
Captain Harnden and his wife and daughters eked out
a living there, wondered where— Mac's yell snapped
me out of my reverie.

"Hey, Bea! Throw her into neutral. I've just snagged
the biggest thing in the sea!"

I tore out on deck so fast I nearly put my foot in the

wash tub of herring. Beth and Bill were bringing in their lines as fast as Mac's was going out. His rod was jumping up and down so vigorously that he put the butt between his legs to steady it. The click of the ratchet became higher and higher in pitch as the line sang out faster. No use touching the reel until this mad run tapered off a bit. He was biting his lips and grinning. "Man, oh man," he chanted, "how he struck. He went after that herring like a cannibal after a missionary." Mac looked around and spoke to Bill quickly, "We're drifting too near the cliff. Head out a little. But do it easy."

The fight was on. There's no arguing with a king. He runs when he feels like it and you can't stop him— unless you want to snap your line or leader—or tear the hooks out of his mouth. Mac hung tight while the charging salmon ripped off two hundred feet of line. Then he stopped and Mac slowly pumped him back to the boat but, when he was near enough to sight it, that king sounded. It had surfaced, the great dorsal fin had cut the water, and then, tail up, it hit for the bottom. The line followed it almost straight down.

"He's halfway to hell and logged down," Mac complained irritably. He lifted the tip of his rod and it bent sharply, but the line never gave an inch. There might have been an anchor instead of a salmon on the end of it.

"The old boy's going to sit this one out. Your move," Bill teased, knowing there was nothing Mac could do. "Cheer up, you've got as much time as he has. But you better be ready when he decides to go to town."

Minutes dragged by. Mac smiled a little lopsided. Yet he was tense and cautious, knowing only a big one would log down like this. He tried gentle, experimental tugs on the line. No luck. He simply had to outwait it.

"Bea," he said, "hear you've been reading up on salmon. I'll try you out. Have I a king, a spring, a chinook, or a tyee on here?"

"Give me a hard one; that's too easy. Those all are different names for the same salmon. Around the Columbia River in Oregon they are known as chinooks, in Washington, as spring or king salmon, and in British Columbia, as tyees. Though Roderick Haig-Brown, an authority on salmon, says that only giants over thirty pounds should properly be called tyee. The Indians sometimes called them sachem. Now they ascend only the larger streams, die after spawning, and—"

"Hold everything!" Mac was shouting as the tip of his rod flew up and the line hung limp. At long last the king had changed his royal mind and was heading toward a commoner. Mac was reeling in fast but there still was no pull on his line. It dangled like wet string. He continued to pump in line and it seemed a full minute later when Bill breathed, "Getting close now, Mac." No one spoke as the reel piled higher; the line still had no tension. Perhaps the salmon had thrown a kink in the stiff leader and snapped it. Maybe the line had parted at some weak spot or perhaps the fish had worked the hooks out. Again, he may have been only lightly hooked. There was no knowing. It was back to beans if that line came in empty. It was cold on deck but Mac was perspiring and chewing his lip.

"Better watch your big-businessman ulcer, Mac," Bill taunted.

"That's your job," Mac snapped, "but I'll get another if—"

He didn't finish, for two things happened at once.

The line whanged taut and instantly flew out again, screaming off the reel, one hundred, two hundred, two hundred and fifty feet at a clip. The reel began to look empty and Mac was no longer perspiring. He was sweating now. He thumbed his reel, hoping to slow that fish down.

"You old tightwad," Bill said, "you've got three hundred feet and you won't even give him a few inches. Let him go. We can follow him in the boat if your line runs too low." Mac grudged out a few more feet while Bill went forward and stood by the wheel, his hand ready on reverse gear.

By the time the king slowed down there was little line left on the reel and the steady hum of the ratchet turned into separate clicks. Bill returned to deck, saying, "Guess that run took the adrenalin out of his liver. He'll come in easily now. But be careful, he may have pulled the hooks loose." We all offered advice. At such a moment, the fisherman who isn't plagued with suggestions is fishing alone.

Mac pumped the fish in, each hard-earned yard rolling on the spool with increasing difficulty. Time after time, he lowered the tip of the rod almost to the water and steadily eased it up, quickly reeling in those precious feet as he lowered it again.

"I tell you, Bill, he's in reverse." He straightened up and rubbed his back with his hand, saying, "What's your best rate for lumbago, Doc?" The line inched in and by now it was so dark we could hardly see where it cut the water. Then we caught the glint of the wire leader and a great back rose up and finned beside the boat. The king rolled once and then shot out like a hound after a rabbit. But it was a final attempt at freedom, a weak one, and it came in quickly until there was only six feet of thread-like wire between Mac and his prize. In the half light, we could see the king roll, see his silver belly flash as he turned. He was spent yet he struggled feebly as Mac led him around for a moment. It takes a lot of doing to dethrone a king. Finally Mac said, "You gaff him, Bill. I'm not that good a sportsman—yet."

We all were hanging over the side of the boat, watching that great salmon lose his last fight. Bill grasped the rail with his left hand and had a death grip on the gaff hook in his right hand. He hovered above that fish— waiting, waiting for just the right second. The salmon, like a wrestler panting for breath and down for the count, slowly fluttered its gill covers that were as big as clam shells. A fighter was humbled. A champion was dying.

Then came the awesome moment when Bill slipped the gaff through a gill and heaved the king over the side. The men cheered as it hit the deck but somehow I didn't feel like cheering. Beth spoke my thoughts, "The King is dead—Long live the King."

The massive body thumped and pounded until Mac rapped it hard at the base of the head; with a head-to-tail shiver, it lay still at our feet. It was a handsome fish, thick and yet well-proportioned. It was over three feet long and perhaps ten inches from the top of that dark green back to the bottom of its silver belly. The head looked like burnished gray metal and the gray, black-spotted tail spread out eight inches.

"That's a real fish, Mac," Bill said, sententiously. "He'll go thirty-three, thirty-six pounds." He squatted down to examine it closely and directed the beam of his flashlight on the numerous sea lice still clinging around the vent.

"Look here. No wonder he fought so hard. He's just fresh in from outside. Sea lice fall off after salmon have been in the Sound for a while. Most of them, that is. Same principle as barnacles falling off in fresh water. They say rivers freshen up the Sound."

Mac was poking his flashlight into the salmon's mouth and he pointed to a rounded, lumpy place between those fearsome teeth.

"That's an old, healed-over hook scar. This king's been snagged before. Some place. Some time."

While the men talked, my thoughts drifted off. I was thinking about the stamina of this valiant king, of his hazardous migration down some river as a fingerling, and how, countless times throughout his life, his instinct had outwitted danger. I wondered where he had spent his days as a wily blackmouth. How many times had his cunning warned him against herring which looked natural but carried hooks? Where had he found the feed to build and nourish that tremendous body and where along the Pacific shelf had he spent his years? If we had not cut his life-span short, would he have ascended the Frazier River in Canada? Or, if his home stream had been the Skagit, would he have made it past the Indians' net at the mouth?

I gazed at him respectfully, wondering what mysterious, unknown instinct was luring him back through hundreds of miles of ocean to the exact pool in the river where he had been spawned four or five years ago. By what magic did he recognize the waters of his own river? Men have different theories concerned with the river's temperature or chemical content or gravitational pull. But only salmon know for sure.

I couldn't feel as exultant as the men even though a sportsman's dream lay at my feet. Considering his weight, the tackle had been light enough to ensure a fair fight. Yet a beautiful thing lay dead. Already his fragile, iridescent scales, smaller and more delicate than those of silver salmon, were losing their gleaming opalescent sheen. The rich deep green of his back was slightly glazed with film and those steel-webbed fins were limp, inert, folded back into useless masses. His powerful tail, which had lashed through the fury of storms and tides, drooped in defeat. In death, the king was robbed of his majesty.

In the cove we anchored, fore and aft. The fish had been cleaned and packed in ice. The men had been very matter-of-fact about the whole thing yet, just before they entered the cabin, I caught Mac standing alone and looking down at that king. Then he raised his hand in silent salute.

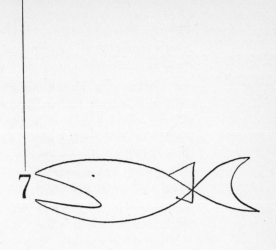

Ethan Allen of Waldron Island

The next morning, when the alarm clock went off at four, its horrible jangle twisted every nerve in my body. I stirred groggily, half dreaming Father Neptune had prodded me with his pitchfork and now was dragging me off to the nether regions in a fire truck, whose clanging bell was announcing our arrival. I opened one eye and closed it again, deciding the whole wide world and all its riches had nothing to offer at the moment.

As with all fishermen, the cold gray dawn and I were old acquaintances—I wouldn't say friends—but there was a reason why I couldn't struggle out this morning. The night before I had glared at that upper bunk of mine as though it were a personal enemy. It had been a comfortable seat-back during the day, but at night when it was chained up into a horizontal position, it felt as though somebody had sneaked the stuffing out and substituted croquet balls. I had made up my mind not to spend a second restless night, so I had taken both halves of a sleeping pill, one half for each hip, a pill I had filched from the samples showered on all physicians. So I had hardly hit that shelf before the lights and I went out together. Since I had never taken one before, that pill hit me like a billy club.

Now the alarm had been turned off but it was like trying to sleep inside a sea-lion cave. Mac was rattling the stove lids and asking Beth where in time she had stowed the coffee. Pots and pans clanked as the boat rolled. Bill must have been sorting and untangling rods and tackle because sinkers that sounded like paving bricks whanged against the cabin roof. Cross, sleepy-eyed children were fighting over whose pants were whose, while Beth, sanely in her bunk, was telling Mac that nobody but night watchmen should be up at this hour.

Half-conscious, I knew I was missing the best fishing time so I dragged my head off the pillow and peered out the open cabin door just a few feet from my head. It was a discouraging sight, for the universe was swathed in battleship-gray mist, the cruiser was tossing, and it looked cold. Right then I wouldn't have left my blankets if a hundred-pound king salmon had jumped aboard, pulled up a frying pan, and sat in it.

As I was about to snuggle down again, I saw something moving on the stern seat. I blinked and looked again. There was somebody in a sleeping bag out there and the head sticking out of it was vaguely familiar. The bronze skin, wrinkled and pouched, appeared mottled in the dim light, and a week's growth of grayish bristles ran into patchy white hair. It was Cappy Bell and he looked worse than a spawned-out salmon. He was on hand for the early fishing.

Just then Bill bustled through the cabin disgustingly cheery.

"Everybody up who's going to fish," he called but grabbed our boys by the shirttails and advised them to stay put until after breakfast. He talked sleepy little Bob into it but had no luck with his elder brother—he might as well have told the tide to sneak gently through Deception Pass. The sensible McKenzie girl slept through all the commotion but Cookie and Dick were up and at 'em.

Mac started the engine and it must have been Bill who heaved up the anchors. The chains, as he coiled them on deck, made a frightful noise. Wincing, I pulled the covers up and let the pill take over.

Several hours later, shouts awoke me. I felt the boat stop, then Mac rushed past me and joined Bill and Cappy, who were jabbering on deck like Indians at a clambake. Young Bill was bouncing up and down and yelling. Evidently he had a fish on, for the men were telling him how to handle the rod that was pounding in his hands.

This was worth watching, so I turned over on my stomach, snuggled the blankets around my neck, and stared out on deck. It was quite a sight. Cappy's parchment face was cracked into a broad, open-toothed smile and his sharp blue eyes were taking in everything. His duck-bill cap was jammed down on his head and he

wore a greasy-slick canvas coat over his scaly blue jeans.
He was perched precariously on the gunwale of the
rolling boat.

"Quit flappin' your fins, boy. Let 'im go," he
coached. "Yuh can't stop him. The way he's runnin'
yuh can tell he's got more gumption than a grizzly's
grandchild. Just be ready when he stops."

The line was whipping out and the child was having
trouble keeping the thumping rod steady. Cappy spoke
up.

"Stick the butt-end of the pole in yuh belly button,
Cookie. I didn't know what-the-hell it was for myself
till I started fishin'.'"

I shuddered, afraid Cappy might unleash his extensive
vocabulary, but my husband had no such worries. He
was beaming at Cappy, happily content to let the master
take over. Cookie hung on and Cappy nodded approval,
saying, "Bound to git fish this mornin'. Never knew it
to fail. The more uncomfortable the fisherman is, the
better the buzzards bite. Fish know. That there king
knew we was hungry 'n cold 'n the boat's rockin' like
a hog in a mud waller. Now, if it was jest a-rainin' an'
we was soaked to the skin, 'n froze stiff an' a good nor'-
easter warmin' up, I'd say we git some fish."

Suddenly Cappy jumped down to the deck, shot the
boy a pained and surprised look, and said, "Sit tight till
I git back." Then he bolted inside the cabin, brushing
past me as he went forward. A moment later he tore
back, stuck his head out the cabin door, and bawled,
"Where in hell do you hide it? Or don't you re-fined
city slickers need 'em?"

Bill was hovering over his son, but he looked back
over his shoulder and laughed, telling Cappy it was 'way

up in the prow. He added, "Hurry back, Old Faithful."

When Cappy returned to deck, he stood at the boy's elbow. Cookie was trying to reel in and making so little progress he foolishly started to tighten the tension on his reel, but Cappy yelled at him so loudly the boy jumped.

"Hey! Leave that alone. Do yuh want him to clean you out of tackle? He'll pull the hook an' beat it. Won't leave no forwarding address, neither. He's jest like me, son. You gotta let him go when he wants to. Now pump him in easy."

While I didn't like his words, I did like his way with the boy and I was thrilled to see this old salt give our son instructions. Cappy showed him how to spread the line evenly on the reel as it came in by using the back of his left thumb. When Cookie let the tip of the rod sink too near the water, Cappy exploded, "Your paw paid good money for the spring in that pole. Why don't yuh use it?"

He explained how the limberness of the pole acted like a spring which broke the full force of the pull and how a bent rod picked up slack instantly, insuring a taut line always.

All of a sudden, Cookie's line fell slack and, though he reeled in as fast as he could, he couldn't keep up with that salmon. Cappy frowned, squinted from the sagging line to the water, and said, "Ain't he a-hellin' in, though?" The men hardly breathed as the line came in close to the boat and dangled almost straight down. They crowded to the rail and then the fish must have surfaced, for they all yelled and pointed excitedly at the water. This was too much, so I half fell out of my upper berth, grabbed a sheepskin coat as I dashed on deck, and elbowed my way to the railing.

Speechless, my jaw fell open. There was a small king all right, but clamped on his tail was a four-foot-long brown thing.

"God. My God, what a cod," Bill was saying, too stunned to move. Mac just stared at it, but Cappy grabbed the gaff hook, braced himself against the rail, and made a lightning jab at the cod, coming up on the under side of it. He held it impaled, shouting, "Git back if you don't want to git yore teeth stove in." We jumped to his bidding, and Cappy, straining and tugging, both hands on the gaff, managed to yank the cod over the side. Its lashing tail upset a chair and sent a pail slithering across the deck. As it thumped and pounded, Cappy glanced at Cookie's line which was ripping off the reel. He said, "Yuh still got him. Hang on tight. Yore on your own for a minute."

I stood in the safety of the cabin doorway, well out of the way of the writhing cod which was throwing himself all over the deck. He was tremendous; his head would have filled a five-gallon pail and his mouth opened up like a Gladstone bag. His great bulging brown eyes were almost as large as a cow's. I remembered that Bill had told me cods' eyes always popped out due to the difference in pressure between the surface and their deep-water habitat.

As Cappy, on his knees, was trying to knock the cod out with a lead pipe, it lunged about convulsively, missing Mac who was standing behind Cookie to protect him, and stung the boy's legs with a slap from its whipping tail. Startled, he let out a yowl but hung onto his rod like an old hand.

The cod, which had not been worn out at all on a line, gave up hard; Cappy pounded him for a long time before he quivered and lay still. It was longer than Cookie was tall, an ungainly lout of a fish with its outsized head and nasty brown skin dotted with big blackish marks. Cappy got up jerkily and shoved it aside with his foot, saying, "There's about seventy pounds of cod for anybody who wants it. I don't." He went over to Cookie and nodded admiringly at the way he was playing his salmon. He slapped him on his shoulder and said heartily, "You're a chip off the old blockhead. Bring it in, son. That cod damn near had salmon tail for breakfast. Easy."

He looked fondly at my husband, winked at him, and made a little clucking noise with his lips. I knew he was approving of our son and, at that moment, I liked Cappy. But just as I was ready to forgive him everything, he pulled a bottle out of his hip pocket, raised it to his mouth, and gurgled down enough to make five cocktails. Then he shook his head, wiped his lips with the back of his hand, and said, "I know it, Doc. The sun ain't crossed the yardarm yet, but this here is just rust-remover. Out in a fog like this, joints git rusty at my age."

Cookie was still playing his fish, his face all smiles. The other children, wakened by the upheaval, were on deck, watching Cookie wear out his king. Poor little Bob's snapping brown eyes were too bright; fretfully he hung onto his father's hand, jumped up and down, and said he wanted a fish, too.

Cappy, waiting to gaff the salmon, said, "That's a right handsome fish, son. A small one. T'won't go over twelve pounds, and if he hadn't had a cod on his tail,

he would have cut some pretty fancy capers. Often
them juniors have more steam than the big hulks. That's
right. Keep his head up. Steady—I've got him."

He dropped the salmon on the deck and solemnly
shook hands with Cookie before handing him the lead
pipe and pliers.

"Your fish. Take care of it," he said. Then Cappy
squinted up at the nine o'clock sun that was attempting
to shine through the mist and drawled, "Fishin' is about
over for this morning. Don't you ever eat around here?"
He rubbed his spare stomach, adding, "I'm flatter'n a
flounder myself."

When Mac said, "Breakfast coming up, Cappy," the
old man glared at me, his look plainly saying that I
should be over the cookstove in the galley where
women belong. Shaking his head sadly, he said to Bill,
"Yuh kin train seals but I dunno about women. I'm
disappointed in yuh, Bill. Yuh ain't made much progress
with her."

My husband laughed. But I didn't. I was cold and
hungry, and before morning coffee, my sense of humor
is at low ebb. Bill says I'm a split personality, two different persons before and after coffee, my B.C. depression unrelated to my A.C. optimism. I flounced into
the cabin, found clothes which resembled mine, and
sought the only possible privacy in the tiny toilet, but it
was like trying to dress in a telephone booth. I skinned
my knuckles stretching into a damp sweater so I stepped
outside to finish, and there the delectable odor of coffee
and bacon breezed through the cabin. Life took on
meaning.

In the galley, Mac was baking his famous pancakes,
so I fell to and set the table while Beth squeezed oranges

and Bill made up the bunks. Just then Dick rushed to
my husband and inquired anxiously if he had any alcohol
in his medical grip.

"Yes, Dick. Why do you want it?"

"To preserve these. A guy at school had a jar of them
and they kept 'most a year." He held out his hand.
Beth and I swallowed hard for he was holding the cod's
gruesome eyes in his fist. Bill left a bunk half made
while he and Dick fixed up the specimen.

Mac called all hands to breakfast when he had a
towering stack of cakes ready, the big thick kind that
stick to your ribs—and other places. The children
swarmed in like locusts to a wheat field. Cookie still
was tingling and aglow but he didn't speak of his fish.
He knew that true fishermen never boast about good
luck. Beth and I fixed the children's plates first, three
cakes apiece, swimming in maple syrup and butter, fruit
juice in paper cups and milk when that was gone. We
shooed them out on deck to eat so there would be room
for the "groans" as they called us grown-ups.

Cappy, smelling of herring, slid into the seat beside
Bill. He didn't bother to remove his hat. He just flipped
the great duck-bill visor up so he could see his plate. We
had thick mugs of steaming, fragrant coffee, and strips
of bacon between each griddle cake, and there was little
conversation at first. We all were hungry enough to eat
the marrow out of bone china. I cooked the second
round which everybody finished except Cappy who left
a half cake on his plate. He sat back and relaxed.

"Eat up, Cappy," I said. "Don't waste that good pan-
cake."

"Nope. I'm through." He slapped a gnarled hand on
the table pushing himself up and said, "I'm not runnin'

anythin' I don't want through my twenty-three feet
jest to please a woman. Besides, I gotta git back and
wet-nurse them herrin' o' mine. Take me ashore, Bill?"

Beth and I opened the portholes after he left and then
went out on deck where the smell of fresh fish was welcome by comparison. At the moment I detested the old
man, and yet a short time ago I had liked him. Couldn't
I ever make up my mind about Cappy?

The children were racing all over the cruiser, jumping about like squirrels, their red life jackets bright in
the sun. Now that the tide had changed, the wind had
gone down and well-behaved little waves feathered
against the rocks of the cove. The mist, clinging low to
the water, was receding into the distance and little boats
would appear from nowhere out of its eery opalescence
as though they had magically emerged from another
world. The high tip of Lummi Island was floating in
the pearly haze, but the tiny Peapod Islands still were
obscured and their sea bell sent out its doleful, woebe-
gone clang, warning mariners of the reefs around there.

Bill, having left Cappy Bell on the beach, returned and
made the dinghy fast with a knot I never could master.
Cookie rushed to his side, saying, "Dad, I want to cook
my fish like the Indians did. You know, bake it in the
sand. Can I, please? Please? It's mine."

After some discussion, Mac said, "Suppose we leave
here and cruise around the east side of Waldron Island.
There's a good beach there and these kids are spoiling
for a run. And we might pick up a blueback or two off
Point Hammond. Tonight we'll eat ashore just as this
young fisherman wants to. How's that?"

With no more ado, Mac heaved anchor and got under
way. Bill herded our sons into the cabin and asked them

to take off their shirts, examining them in his clinical manner. Cookie had no temperature nor any new poxes and the old ones were drying up. He was over the hump, but Bob had a slight fever.

"Only a couple of new poxes, fella," he said. Turning to me, he automatically assumed his professional voice, "I'd keep him perfectly quiet for a day or so."

How often I'd heard him say this over the telephone to anxious mothers, just as though he knew what it meant to keep a restless, fretful child "perfectly quiet." I had yearned for this moment.

"Fine," I answered, airily, "let's see you do it." With a challenging smile I breezed to the galley and stacked the dishes.

But darned if he didn't. He tucked Bob down beside him on a bunk and began telling him a fascinating "war story." He told the boy there was a fierce battle going on right that minute in his body: two great opposing forces were fighting in his blood. The valiant white cells, under the leadership of Captain Corpuscle, were attacking the chicken pox germs, and his slight fever just proved how hot the skirmish was. He explained that Captain Corpuscle was a doughty old warrior and would surround the enemy, but that he could do it lots quicker if the battlefield was quiet.

"Who's going to win, Daddy?" Bob's eyes were wide and alarmed.

"Oh, Captain Corpuscle, by all means. He almost always does, though it may take him several days to gather enough recruits. As he needs them, a base called 'bone marrow' will send out fresh regiments." I listened to the story as it went on about how the intrepid Captain was throwing up barracks which were the poxes themselves and how hard it was for the heart to pump fresh soldiers to the line of battle. Gradually Bill's voice became lower and lower and finally he stopped speaking. Bob was asleep. It was my turn to eat crow.

By noon we were skirting the north shore of Orcas Island, giving treacherous Parker's Reef a wide berth. On our starboard, several miles away, Sucia Island lazed in the sunshine, and beyond it was Patos Island with its beacon light. Ahead lay Waldron Island across deep and swift President's Channel. After lunch, the children were willing to take naps, all except Bob who had had his sleep out. But he was quietly content to nestle down in his father's lap and half hold the rod Bill had put out. Beth and I were fishing, too. There was only a small chance of catching kings in the daytime so we saved Cappy's herring for evening fishing. Though they were dead, they could be limbered up and used.

Mac had helped us rig our lines with canned three-inch herring more suitable in size for the bluebacks we hoped to get. Under his direction we attached single steelhead hooks to eighteen inches of leader wire and then worked the tip of the wire through the vent of each herring. We pulled the leader through the mouth until the shank of the hook was well inside the herring's body and only the curved part with the barb and tip exposed protruded from the vent. We had then fastened the leader to an eight-inch silver flasher which was attached to the cuttyhunk by another eighteen inches of leader wire.

Beth was fishing near the surface with only twenty-five feet out above her slip sinker; I let out fifty feet and went down deeper. Bill had piled on lead and was fishing way down so we were working three levels.

We trolled for an hour off Point Hammond with Mac at the wheel. He was having his hands full trying to keep in fairly close and yet avoid the kelp beds. We could see bubbles break on the surface of the water so we knew herring were there. Occasionally we saw one flip out of the riffling waves. Gulls were circling overhead. There was bait here all right. The big midsummer run of silver salmon wasn't in but there were a few around and, like bluebacks, they are more of a tide fish than kings for they bite all day long, though generally best when an incoming tide brings in herring. Silver fishing is apt to be hottest when low slack and an incoming tide comes in the early morning or late evening, the natural feeding time for fish.

We were sitting in a row, slumped down in comfortable canvas deck chairs, our legs stretched out on the stern seat. No worries, no cares—not even children at the moment. It was a crystal cool yet warm June day and we drank in the land-sweet breeze that smelled so deliciously of warm earth and cedar, spiced with salt air. The island-locked sea was gentian blue, the distant Canadian mountains hazy powder blue in contrast to Mount Baker and the Three Sisters peaks which were radiantly white. There were no other boats in sight; we "owned" this beautiful bit of the world, tailor-made for a sportsman.

Between lovely long silences, Beth and I chatted about cats and cabbages and kings and lots of less important things. Bill was quiet but happily so, and even Bob was content.

Then, when we reeling in to inspect our lines, Beth had a strike. A good one. With the swashing flashers— needed to attract attention to our bait herring which looked like all the others—the tips of the rods always vibrated gently, but hers had snapped. The line came in limp with only a mangled herring to prove she'd had a nibble. Bill showed her how to cut the leader off close to the flasher and thread on a fresh herring from the jar. Beth wrinkled her nose as he carefully worked the leader wire through the vent and out the mouth and then twisted the wire back onto the swivel attached to the flasher. Bill explained that, after four or five rebaitings, she would have to put on a new leader as it lost an inch or so each time. But he swore it was worth the trouble —that this setup outfished spoons or plugs every time. He repolished the flasher and heaved the rig overside.

My herring looked sort of bedraggled and weary, and rather than go through that highly personal business of rebaiting, I decided to switch to a nice new plug. Anyway, whatever fish were around didn't seem to crave herring at the moment and a cagey fisherman changes bait when one kind does not work.

My brand-new three-inch herring-scale plug was still in its box on a shelf in the cabin. I tiptoed in so as not to wake the other children and pawed around on the loaded shelf. But with difficulty I swallowed the yell that rose up in my throat when I saw two great brown eyes glaring at me malevolently from their jar. Alcohol had not softened the expression in that cod's eyes one bit and I fervently wished Cappy had taken them along with the rest of the cod, to shore.

Back on deck, my plug's yellow bead eyes looked guileless indeed. I cut a six-foot leader from the big coil of leader wire and twisted the plug on, using a double loop to insure free action. Then I attached the other end to the swivel on the crescent sinker. It was a relief not to monkey with a flasher—plugs are so different in action flashers are not often used. That "hardware" dragged on the line and, too, the weight took some of the play out of the fish. My peppy little plug would have enough appeal without it.

Bill eased Bob off his lap as he stood up and watched me test out my plug. It did have a quick, lively swimming action, but it didn't dart out sideways every once in a while as it should have done.

"No good," Bill said. "Bring it in and I'll adjust the eye that holds the leader." With pliers, he bent the tiny staple a wee bit to one side and we tried it again. It worked beautifully. It still had that enticing, provocative wiggle but now it also shot out to one side occasionally as a herring would when being chased.

"Try that," he murmured, lazily sitting down again and drawing Bob to his knee. "That looks good but you never can tell what will tempt a fish. I wouldn't trade you a dozen plugs for that tooth-marked baby I found on the beach. I've caught a round dozen salmon on that coughed-up plug. It's got plenty of oomph."

Lines out, we all settled back, and Beth asked Bill what the bluebacks around here really were.

"Well," he drawled, "fishermen don't agree. Experts say it's a green or immature silver salmon—and of course you know that Canadians call a silver salmon a coho. Same fish, 'nother name. But bluebacks are sort of a riddle; they don't run with silvers, their meat is always very red, and I've caught 'em dead ripe, ready to spawn. If they are silvers, their backs must change from blue to silver-gray in a mighty short time and true silvers often have pale pink meat.

"Curly Cramer at West Beach Resort has seen tons of

fish brought in, and he insists the meat resembles a sockeye and that they are sold to canners for sockeyes. But
of course a sockeye never takes a hook. Guess he feeds
on different food or perhaps he couldn't open his prissy
little mouth wide enough to snag a hook.

"Now, Granpaw Anthony on Orcas knows fish
coming and going, and he says it's a specie by itself.
Damned if I know what they are and I don't care as
long as they like my herring."

But right then, a salmon preferred my plug!

There was a good swift jerk on the line before it
whizzed out and the ratchet sang the fisherman's favorite tune.

"Fish on, Mac. Stop the engine," Bill called. Beth
and he were reeling in to give me the field when my fish
jumped.

"Holy suffering Moses," I panted as it shot into the
air. "He'll kink my leader for sure and—"

"Hey," Bill shouted as though I were in the next
county, "keep him away from that kelp bed. He's heading for it and he'll get all tangled up." But the run
stopped short and I was reeling in a fighting mad fish.

"You're not so smart," I gloated. "Pretty soon I'll
have a tooth-marked plug of my own."

"Mebbe," Bill answered, watching a streak of silver
dart up several feet into the air, "and-maybe-not. Don't
forget we have a propeller if he goes under the boat."

After that jump, my line came in slack and my spirits
wilted. But a few seconds—and fifty feet of line—later,
the tip of my rod jerked down. Shining-eyed Bob was
excited, too excited for his own good. He was jumping
up and down at my elbow, chanting, "Get it, Mommie,
get it."

This time, I could keep up with it as it came toward the boat. But there was no stopping that salmon as it tore under the cruiser, bending my rod to a killing curve. The tip was under water and I thought it must snap.

"Feed it around the stern," Bill cried, "and quickly." He shoved me up onto the stern seat and I made a wide sweep with the bent rod, praying the line would clear the rudder. It must have, for now I was fishing from the other side of the boat, line and fish having passed beneath it. There was a nice long smooth run and I had a moment to exult. I loved that exciting tingle that ran up the line to the rod and right on into my spirits. This was a battle of wits, his against mine, and anybody could win. Did that salmon out there have a future—or only a past? If he were lightly hooked, could I ever bring him in? Would he tear the hooks out by prying against the plug itself? But I had him. So far.

Again he jumped, perhaps more horizontally than a steelhead, but the splash as he socked the water sounded just the same. He had tossed his head violently in an effort to dislodge the hooks and that thwack on the surface might have helped.

Slowly, I brought him in, wondering if each turn of the reel might prove too much for the grip of the hooks. Then we saw his blue back as he raced along beside the boat. Bill put the net down, but the salmon wasn't ready to give up yet. He made two more stabs at freedom, short frantic runs, before he came in and half floated beside us. He gasped only a couple of times before Bill swished the net under him and swung him aboard. On the deck, still in the net, he thrashed and thumped around, tangling the flying hooks into the mesh. It was hard to avoid those darting hooks and grasp him by the back so as to knock him out with our trusty lead pipe reserved for such rituals.

"Go ahead, he's your fish," Bill smiled complacently and sat down again. He let out his line as Mac started the engine. It was a terrible job working those two triple hooks out of the mesh, and the salmon had wound himself up in the leader. When he was free, I proudly showed Bill how lightly he had been hooked—only one prong of one hook was loosely lodged in the soft corner of his mouth. I tried to appear offhand as I placed it in the zinc-lined fish box that also held Cookie's and Mac's kings.

Bill looked thoughtfully at the three salmon for a moment and then reeled in, saying, "I think I'll clean him now. It's warm out here. The ice is about melted and we have two fish ahead of him to eat first. He'll have to wait his turn. He'll keep better if I clean him now."

"What do you mean, you'll clean him? He's my fish!" Bill looked at me and we both burst out laughing but quickly assumed sober faces as we played our Tom Sawyer-Huckleberry Finn game for Bob's benefit. We always pretended to fight over who had the "privilege" of cleaning each fish. Our deluded sons thought it was an honor and fought to do it, suiting us just fine. As we expected, Bob spoke up quickly, "Mommie, please. I get to clean him. Please."

"No, sonny, not this time," Bill said, stifling a chuckle. "You're sick but you may help me if Mother will only let me do it. Will you, dear?" I debated but finally gave in to their pleadings. It was hard to keep a straight face.

Beth had spread newspapers on the deck and was on her knees watching Bill slit open the blue-backed fish. He took the gills out, knowing fish keep better that way, and he was careful not to rupture the inside membrane lining the body cavity. Bob was on his knees, too, still resentful over my "favoritism." His dark head was close to Beth's blonde hair. In her cherry-colored sweater and navy blue slacks she was very pretty and she had that wide-eyed innocent look which seems to go with blondes.

Bill was tugging at the fish's innards and pulled out a long flatish slab of immature roe and tossed the mass of tiny eggs to one side.

"What's that, Daddy?"

"Those are fish eggs, Bob."

"Do all fish have eggs?"

"No. Just the mother fish."

"What do the daddies have?" Bob asked, puzzled.

"Oh," Bill answered absently, busy trying to clean the clotted blood from the triangular sack under the backbone. "The daddy fish have milch. They swim over the eggs after the mother lays them and fertilize them."

"He uses fish fertilizer on the eggs?" Bob asked, incredulous. "Do all daddies use fertilizer?"

"Uh huh, sort of," Bill evaded.

"But daddy," the boy persisted, "did you—?"

Bill ran his fingers through his hair, completely forgetting they were covered with fish blood. It was the first time I'd ever seen him at a loss for words. He opened his mouth, shut it, glowered at his vastly amused female audience, and finally beat a hasty retreat to the cabin.

An hour later we were peacefully trolling along the lovely east side of Waldron when the children woke up. After their naps, they were full of bounce and beans—

Mexican jumping beans—and they tore out on deck. Cookie took one look at the beautiful cove we were passing and cried excitedly, "That's it, Mommie. That's where I want to cook my salmon. In the sand like Cappy Bell showed you. Can't we kids please go ashore?" All the children shouted at once and Dick pulled in the painter on the dinghy.

It was a veritable story-book bay snugged down between two protecting rocky arms. At the head of it there was a crescent of sandy beach where salt-bleached driftwood gleamed in the sunshine. The serious-minded dark green of the firs in the background was brightened here and there by the shiny lighter green of madrona trees. It was a love of a place and there was no sign of habitation.

Bill was at the wheel now so we held a powwow in the cabin. Mac said we needed more ice and fresh milk, too. He said there was good fishing almost all the way to the little town of Orcas where supplies could be procured. So, to the children's deafening delight, it was decided that I would take them ashore and start baking the big salmon in the sand while the boat went on. Beth elected to stay on the criuser, perhaps less for the joy of fishing than to be rid of supercharged youngsters, but I was anxious to try my hand at Cappy's "recipe."

Beth and I gathered all the food and cooking utensils we would need and I spurned Mac's suggestion of taking newspaper for kindling. Cookie's eyes clouded with storm signals when we wrapped Mac's fish, not his, for cooking on the beach. But his father drew him aside and told him that the mark of a true sportsman is conservation and not waste of food and that we'd have his salmon tomorrow. That helped—a little. So the oldest of the three fish was passed down to me in the dinghy. After his father had whispered something into Bob's ear, that droopy little fellow was willing to stay on the cruiser and I wondered if he had promised him the *Queen Mary*. His lassitude worried me; I hoped Captain Corpuscle was doing his stuff.

Mac already had rowed the three elder children ashore and now I was nearing the sandy beach, the huge salmon cuddled in my arms like a baby. The water at this tide was so shallow I had to take off my shoes and socks and wade in—in to the Land of Oz. Never had I seen such an enchanting place. Gnarled and twisted firs grew on top of those high rocky cliffs which were dappled with shadows reflected from the water. The children were clambering over boulders and calling to me that they had discovered a cliff swallow's long mud nest. The gull-splashed ledge was dangerously high, but I tried to remember that children, like the mules they often resemble, are wonderfully sure-footed. At the moment I didn't disturb their ecstasy, but I would call them back to the beach when my nerves wore too thin. Anyway, here was a chance to put into practice my pet theory that, if children can let off steam naturally on thrilling but reasonably safe adventures, they won't crave less desirable escapades. Youngsters thrive on a little danger in their diet.

So I turned my back on them and laid the salmon down on a huge silver driftwood log and started to dig a long narrow trench in the dry sand well above high-tide mark. When it was deep and long enough to suit a king of such majestic proportions, I looked about for kindling. Dry, crinkly seaweed would be just the thing, but ten matches later I decided it would not burn, so I resorted to cedar splinters.

The children had returned to the water's edge and were busy prying great purple starfish off the base of the rocks, so I could relax in peace, only coming out of my trance occasionally to toss another piece of bark on the fire. But suddenly the silence was shattered. Barbara was running down the shore toward me screaming, her pigtails flying out behind her. In the background the boys were doubled over, laughing. When she threw herself in my arms, I discovered that the horny pincers of several crabs were gripping her blonde pigtails. I tried to soothe her by showing how cute the crabs were and that they just nipped a bit and really didn't hurt. I washed the tears off her rosy little face with sea water and soon she ran back to the boys—with the crabs in her pocket.

Minutes passed, as smoothly as silver beads on a chain. The smoke from the glowing bark fire curled lazy and blue against the rock wall. I was alone, but not lonely. In a world of blue and green, the terra cotta bark of the madrona tree was a lovely splash of color. Gray-winged, white-breasted sea gulls circled over the water, occasionally remaining suspended and inert in mid-air, a living kite with gravity the string. Such beauty was good company.

I was pulling in long kelp streamers to wrap the fish in when I looked up to see an old gentleman walking toward me. For a moment I just gaped at him, then I was embarrassed, realizing we were poaching on someone's land without having known it.

As the stately old islander came closer, I went to meet him, thinking up a quick and sincere apology. Already

I could see his blue eyes under a great thatch of white hair and they seemed to be kindly. The slow, measured way he walked, the way he stepped lightly on the beach as though he loved it, and his smile all spoke of gentleness.

"I'm sorry we're trespassing on your land," I blurted out just as Cookie and Dick rushed toward us, snickering at catching a grown-up in a tight spot. But the boys didn't know what to make of it when the man dropped an arm affectionately around each of their shoulders.

"You're not trespassing," he said quietly. "This isn't my land. These are God's acres and I'm just lucky enough to use them for my lifetime. Anybody is welcome to the Lord's estate. Sit down, all of you, and tell me your names. It's nice to have callers."

He was a handsome old man, his face dignified and serene. The lines around his mouth and eyes must have been etched by a million smiles. His faded blue jeans and shirt were worn into comfortable grooves, too.

"We're going to bake salmon in the sand like the Indians did," Cookie said, spilling out the words eagerly. Our host sat down on a log, thoughtfully crossed his legs, and said mildly, "Somebody's been fooling you. Indians barbecued their salmon." Both lads were crunched down in the sand at the man's feet, as drawn to him as I was. Little Barbara stood shyly to one side.

"Say, will you show us how to cook it as the Indians did? Just exactly?" Cookie asked, sensing with a child's intuition that he was speaking to a friend.

"I'd like to. But first, let's get acquainted. I'm Ethan Allen."

"The guy who lived during the Revolution?" Dick

stammered, and then hung his head when we all laughed at him.

"No. But he was my ancestor. Or at least, my mother said he was and that good woman never lied. No, son, I've been living here on Waldron Island for fifty years, teaching school and collecting Indian relics. And friends. Now about that fish. See the tall rangy bush growing on the bank over there? That's called Ocean Spray or Hardhack, and the Indians discovered that it splits true, right down the center." He asked the boys their names and I introduced myself and Barbara, who climbed up on his knee. I told him how delighted we were to have his help and asked him if he had time to join our dinner party. Before he answered, he handed Cookie his jack-knife and told him to cut two pieces of Hardhack, one as big around as his thumb, the other as large as his wrist, and both of them taller than he was. Then he told Dick just where his cabin was up in the woods and where to look for a long thin sharp knife. When both boys raced off, he turned to me and said, "Of course I have time to join your party. I'm lucky. I have time for everything. And, you know, I'm enjoying my old age. I'm finding answers to a lifetime of questions." He smiled down at Barbara and stroked her hair, saying softly, "I've learned a lot in seventy-five years and one thing I know for sure. If a person does his best, ultimately everything will turn out for his own good." He looked up at me, his eyes twinkling. "Course I don't do much now but read and think. But at that, I'm a busy man. You see, by the time I get the tide in in the morning and out again in the afternoon, the whole day's shot. Seems like—"

The boys descended on him with what they imagined were Indian war whoops. They had smeared red clay from the bank over their faces and stuck sea gull feathers in their hair.

"What tribe you from, boys?" he chuckled, examining the poles Cookie handed him. "Now I'll show you what the Indians did."

As he split the smaller slender pole lengthwise, he told us about the days when he was superintendent of all the island schools way back before the turn of the century.

"Yes, sir," he said, "I clucked over those one-room schools like a mother hen, and every few months I made the round of all of them—in a rowboat. By actual count, boys, I've rowed ten thousand miles and I had some pretty close shaves, too. I was paid one hundred dollars a year. This farm fed us, so that was clear, and I would have been in the white-collar class—if I'd had one." He picked up the two clean-cut halves of poles and said, "Now where's your fish?"

He unwrapped it, removed the head and tail, and while he trimmed away the great fins and their cartilaginous bases, he told us about his collection of Indian relics: about the toy canoe carved from a wolf's tooth, and the perfection of his rock-chipped arrow tips.

"Wonderful people, those early Indians," he said. "Why, the canoes they hollowed out of fifty-foot logs were true to a fraction of an inch. And what good fishermen they were."

Now he was filleting the salmon, inserting the tip of the long knife between the large rib bones and the flesh. Skillfully he ran the knife its full length along the ribs, cutting close to them from the backbone toward the belly. He did this on both sides of the salmon until the bare ribs stood up separate from the great chunks of meat that peeled back. Then he cut down past the backbone on each side, careful not to pierce through the skin at the ridge of the back, and lifted out the whole bone structure. The boneless fillets opened out like the leaves of a book. The chunk was about two feet long and nearly as wide. The meat was coral-red.

"I like this red salmon best," he said, "though it doesn't taste a mite better than the white and some folks say it isn't as good. But I like this color 'cause it looks like the sky in a first-rate sunset. Now, hand me those sticks."

He made stretchers out of the half-rounded green sticks, measuring each section against the width of the salmon before he cut it. Then he wedged the ends of the sticks securely into the skin at the outer edge of the chunk. He used eight of them, all on the flesh side of the salmon to be sure it would stay flat and not curl in the heat. He then picked up the stout pole and split it down only two feet and inserted the spread-out salmon between the prongs of this holder. The open ends flared apart several inches.

"Now, boys," he said, "we could easily wire these two ends together which would clamp the fish in nice and tight. But we're doing everything the way the Indians did—and of course they didn't know about wire. What do you 'spose they used? Think now, what won't burn easily?"

He gave them plenty of time to guess. There was nothing hurried about Ethan Allen and I sensed he had so ordered his whole life that there was no need for haste and confusion. Advanced age had given him the luxury of leisure but his years of rowing with the tides had taught him to work with, never against, the inevitable.

He smiled when the boys finally gave up and they

followed him as he climbed the bank behind us. I watched him go to a young cedar tree and strip the stringy bark off one side. He trailed this to the water's edge and thoroughly soaked it, then spread it on a log and pounded it with a rock until the green bark was macerated. Next he doubled it in half, twisting it into sort of a rope which he tied around the ends of the gapping stick which sandwiched the salmon.

Ethan Allen added more bark to the fire and, when it had burned down to red embers, he stuck the end of the long pole into the sand at a sharp angle and braced it with rocks so that the clamped fish was held about a foot above the coals, skin side toward the fire.

"There," he said, "that ought to do it. The Indians used to baste it with sea water to keep it from drying out. That's good, and I've done it several times when I was storm-bound on some uninhabited island. Always took my fishing pole with me. Then I knew I'd never starve. Trolled as I went, so if mean weather came up, I was all set.

"But back to basting this critter. Now these Indians were pretty smart people and if they'd had lemons and butter and garlic, they would have used them instead of sea water. C'mon, I'll get some."

The children trailed him to his cabin and Ethan Allen soon returned with a cupful of mixed orange, lemon juice, and melted butter. He pointed to the white slivers that floated on top, saying, "There's nothing so good but that a bit of garlic doesn't make it better."

I thanked him and said I hoped it wouldn't deprive him, for it must be hard to get fresh food on this island.

" 'Tis," he smiled, "but the harder you come by a thing, the nicer it is to share with friends." He added

more fir bark to the smoldering fire before basting the
salmon with a tablespoonful of the mixture. It sizzled
and smelled wonderful. We all scooped seat holes in the
sand and sighed contentedly as we leaned back against
the big cedar log.

"How did the Indians catch salmon, Mr. Allen?"
Dick asked.

"Well, son, they speared them or used cedar-bark nets.
But the way they caught cod is mighty clever." He
glanced at the boys and was sure of his audience; they
were as intent as owls, their eyes popping out of the red
clay rings around them.

"Dick, go bring me that long piece of kelp over
there." When the boy handed it to him, Ethan Allen
slipped his hands along its twenty feet, working away
from the bulbous head toward the slender end about the
thickness of a lead pencil. He asked Dick to break it.
The child strained and tugged but the kelp did not part.

"The Indians knew it wouldn't break easily, too, so
they used it for a fish line. They tied a small fish, maybe
a trout or a rock cod, onto the tip of a piece of kelp with
a braided grass cord through the gills. Then they put a
stone in the fish's mouth."

"What for?" we all asked in chorus.

"To weight it down, like we use a sinker. Now cod
are often found near kelp beds, so they paddled their
canoes to the edge of one and dangled their kelp lines
down deep. They didn't have to gig it very long before
the bait fish attracted a big ling cod. Ever see one?"
Cookie and Dick excitedly agreed they had.

"Well, when a ling cod grabbed that fish, of course
the Indian felt it on the kelp line and pulled it up until
the cod broke water, still on the tail of that bait fish.

Sometimes a big one swallowed it whole. Then all the Indian had to do was to spear the cod. Wasn't that smart?"

He told us many more stories while the salmon cooked and the sun arched its way toward the western horizon behind us. Never have I peeled potatoes and shelled peas more happily. My soul was simmering in its own juices. The trees made long shadows now and the light was growing deeper, richer, more golden. Ethan Allen basted the fish again and turned the pole that held it, so that now it was flesh side toward the fire.

"Have to watch close, boys. Just want it a golden brown."

It was after seven. The cruiser soon would be back, so I raked a flat place on the coals and put the potatoes on to cook. As I leaned over, a strand of hair fell into my eyes and I brushed it back with a hand that smelled decidedly fishy. Fish is grand but anything fishy is terrible. Instantly, my mind flashed back to Hannah: "A lady never smells, neither good nor bad." All during my childhood that had ruled out perfume, but now it ruled out fish, so I scrubbed my hands hard in the wet sand. I looked up to see the boat nosing into the bay.

Now the salmon was turned skin-side down for its final cooking, and it was basted often. The aroma was so tantalizing it nearly drove us crazy, and hungry little Barbara leaned over it and sniffed and sniffed. The peas were cooking and the coffee pot was on. Sea gulls, getting wind of the fish, circled and cried above us.

As Bill was rowing Beth and Bob ashore in the dinghy, Cookie looked up admiringly at Ethan Allen and said, "Gee, you know so much. Bet you went to college."

"Yes, sir, I did," the old gentleman said thoughtfully.

"Right here on Waldron Island. Nights. For my fresh-
man year, I went through Redpath's *History of the
World*. My first son arrived when I was a sophomore,
and my wife and I were so hard up that all I could afford
to buy was Webster's *Dictionary*. That was spotty reading, but good. My junior term I studied Huxley's *Ani-
mal Biology*, and I topped off my senior year with all of
Dickens' works, just to be sure about what made people
tick. Of course, I borrowed lots of books, but those
were the only ones I owned at the time. That meant
I had to do a heap of thinking about each one. That's
all college can do for you, make you think. Yes, Cookie,
I went to college."

Bob ran up the beach toward me, yelling that we were
going to have ice cream for dessert. Later, when Bill
had brought Mac to shore, Dick and Cookie pounced on
their fathers who pretended to cringe from the painted,
feathered warriors. I was hovering over the fire, making
sure the potatoes were done and the peas just right.
Ethan Allen introduced himself to the men and then
removed the salmon from over the coals. The children
were dancing in anticipation as he improvised a driftwood table and laid the steaming fish on it. With a fork,
he pried up the crispy-dry stretchers. There lay the
salmon.

Beside the peas and potatoes on each plate, he gave us
each helpings of fish we thought we never could finish—
great mounds of delicately pink meat, juicy and golden
brown on top.

That fish! There is only one thing that can improve
the flavor of salmon basted with lemon juice and butter
and that's smoke—only a hint of it, but the tang brought
out all the rich sweetness of the salmon. It tasted better

than anything I'd ever had in my life, far superior to salmon steamed in the sand. Mac licked his lips, loosened his belt, and helped himself to more, and soon all of us did the same. We never would forget that meal.

It was nearly dark when we finished eating. Dick rowed out for the ice cream aboard the cruiser while our host poured out his "high-gear" coffee. He said it was no good unless it would float an ax head. This coffee would all right, but it tasted mighty good around the camp fire. After second and third cups, the men cleaned up and burned the paper dishes while the children rolled over on their backs, fairly groaning they were so full.

I asked Ethan Allen what he knew about the origin of the San Juan Islands.

"About a million years ago, more or less, Mother Nature must have given herself an awful heave and shifted a whole chain of coastwise mountains, toppled 'em over on their sides. Then glaciers oozed down from Alaska and gouged out deep valleys and later the sea rushed in. Tides curled and swirled around the projecting rocks and gradually turned stone to sand. In time, there was vegetation and good soil developed." He pointed with his thumb back over his shoulder, adding, "For instance, it took a hundred thousand years to form that bank. Shells prove it."

He continued talking in his low voice, telling us how different each island is from the other, all with separate personalities. San Juan Island is flatish, long and narrow; Orcas Island is mountainous and nearly halved by East Sound so that it resembles a horseshoe. He said most of the islands were forested, others, partially so, with only a thin epidermis of soil on top of their solid rock—just enough for a pocketful of garden here and there. Most of the islands have people living on them, some only one or two families, and he told us stories about them. At one point, Cookie interrupted him, asking how the islands ever had been divided between the United States and Canada.

"That's a very interesting story," he said, "one that every diplomat in the world should know about. Well, if the borderline between Canada and the United States had been continued in an imaginary straight line, it would have cut straight through some of these islands. Even politicians were smart enough to know that wouldn't work, so, in 1873, they thought up a real good plan. Since the Canadian Frazier River has its mouth near the boundary line between the two countries, it was decided that the shortest distance from the mouth of the river to the Strait of Juan de Fuca would be a logical international line dividing the islands.

"This was fine with both sides, so rival British and American ships started out from the river mouth to log the shortest distance possible. But it was only natural that the United States expedition chose to veer upward and go through Haro Strait as that route would give us more islands. And I'm mighty glad they did, for they just managed to squeeze Waldron Island in—the boundary line's about a mile from the western shore.

"Now the British captain was doing some figuring, too, and he planned to claim more islands for England by dropping down a little. Well, the payoff came when the charts and logs were studied. In nautical miles, both routes were almost identical and, worse still, each marked a sensible line of division. This didn't settle a thing, so the records were given to Kaiser Wilhelm of Germany to arbitrate as a disinterested party. Thank goodness, he chose the American route as the most logical—and so the line stands today."

Ethan Allen reached out and poked the fire into a shower of sparks and chuckled, "The English took it in good grace but one of them said, 'Give the damn Yankees the islands; the salmon won't rise to the fly anyway.'"

Mac asked him what was the most important export from these islands. He mentioned dairy products and eggs and timber, and then held up a finger and shook it at us.

"But do you know what our most valuable crop is?" No one answered.

"It's the people themselves. You see, we can afford the luxury of kindness. Nobody's going to be grabby and jealous when there's so much of everything, so much space and water and fertility. The sea offers up as much food as the land. Mother Nature is mighty good to us around here, and living on an island makes you neighborly. In the San Juans it doesn't take money to be happy. It just takes time—time to enjoy your freedom. And, you know, freedom to do what's right for you is contentment. Now isn't it?"

It was late; the stars were higher now. We didn't say a thing to break the spell except to thank Ethan Allen. As we rowed back to the cruiser we listened to the water whisper and gurgle under the keel and our wake was outlined in phosphorescent sparks.

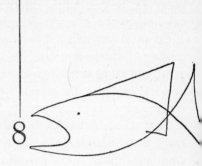

8

Hook, line, and stinker

"Come and get 'em, hot," Mac was bellowing in his bull-seal voice. Half awake, I smelled the beckoning fragrance of coffee, heard the children scampering about topside, and felt the steady thrumming of the engines which I dreamily imagined to be the heartbeat of the sea. Water that ebbed and flowed, and was so full of life, should have a pulse. I stole another minute to listen to the singing swish and slap of water rippling away from the prow. It's an enchanting sound—unless it means you are leaving a place you love. At the moment the water whispered sadly. I hated to pull away from Waldron Island.

Feeling guilty, I joined the others who were already

lined up in the galley, plates and cups in hand. The youngsters were looking at Mac and his stack of hot-cakes with wide, anticipatory grins. Cookie, his cheeks a little too smudged to kiss, had his eyes on the food, but Bob snuggled up against me. I kissed his forehead and was greatly relieved to feel it cool and normal.

"Thought you couldn't sleep on a boat," Beth taunted, smiling at me over the coffee she was pouring. She looked so pretty that I felt a twinge of jealousy; her snug blue jeans and sweater were just like mine but she had better reasons for wearing them.

Bill was at the wheel, so I gulped my food and took him a pile of pancakes that resembled the Leaning Tower of Pisa.

"Morning, dear. Where you been? Get out the chart, will you?"

We were heading north, up President's Channel, and in the morning sunshine the sea shimmered like green watered silk. Portside, the Canadian islands and mountains were poking out of a blue haze and to starboard, Mount Baker was serene and white. A few miles ahead of us were Patos, Sucia, and Matia Islands, green forests which had gone to sea in their youth.

Between bites, Bill spread the chart before him and pointed to the island whose deep bays and narrow ridges of land made it appear like a giant's outspread hand.

"That's Sucia Island—it lies straight ahead. Notice this reef right here?" He was indicating a place on the chart a bit west and south of Sucia where there were only a few fathoms of water.

"That's a kelp bed. You'll generally find it growing on such reefs." Bill went on to explain that it must have been put there by Davy Jones to keep greenhorn

mariners out of his locker. Bill said areas around kelp
beds are generally excellent fishing, because herring seek
the protection of those long, fluted streams, only to
draw their arch enemy, the salmon, after them.

"Look," he nodded ahead to the fluttering white
specks in the distance. "Gulls are working over that
reef right now. Herring are there, all right. Business
should be good tonight." He suggested I study that tiny
reef near Sucia and pick out the best place to fish. I
pored over it for a while and then pointed to a place
where the fathom markings jumped from three to
twenty-four.

"There. That's it," I said. "Big ones should lurk in
that deep, fairly quiet water, waiting for the herring to
dart out of the kelp above. Also, it's protected by being
in the lea of the incoming tide. Am I right?"

"Yep. Should be good." He smiled at me and winked,
"You're learnin'." He told me that, even if you knew
all the tricks of the trade, it was a lead-pipe cinch you
couldn't catch fish if they weren't there, that they come
in with some tides and not with others. Also, that the
lure which is hot on Tuesday and knocks 'em dead on
Wednesday may leave them cold on Thursday.

"But there's some science and sense to the racket at
that. I know it's true that a *good* fisherman, over a
period of time, outfishes the amateur."

I took my trick at the dishpan, for Beth had helped
with breakfast. Curled up on a bunk, she read out loud
from a book on the geology of the San Juan Islands.

"Hey, Bill," she yelled above the noise the children
were making in the forward cabin, "betcha didn't know
we're in the middle of a submerged mountain range."

"Do tell." I was brusque, more engrossed in washing

a griddle four times bigger than the sink than I was in natural history. I also was wondering what in the world the youngsters could be doing. It sounded as though they were moving a hardware store in a dump truck. Just then they all clanked into the galley, dragging picks, two shovels, and assorted chisels. Barbara was banging two pails together.

"What's up?" I demanded, thinking it was more restful to have your front teeth filed than to spend a week on a cruiser with four children. Cookie spoke condescendingly, "I 'spose you 'groans' don't know there are swell fossils on Sucia. We're going to dig 'em." Indian file, they rattled out to the afterdeck.

Mac took the wheel as we neared Sucia. An experienced hand was needed to nose a passage between the reefs and tiny islands which make up this baby archipelago. He gave all kelp a wide berth and headed down Fossil Bay which is only a few hundred yards across. Evergreens grew atop the cliffs beside us, but at the head of the long, narrow inlet, was a crescent beach. We slipped past great slabs of smooth rock two stories high. Now we could see bottom. When the anchor plopped down, it took all sense of time and trouble with it. This beautiful cloistered place must be the anteroom of heaven. In jig time, the children tumbled into the dinghy with all their crashing implements.

"Tell you, Bill," Mac said, "we'll stay here until just before slack water at five tonight. Then we'll hit it back to that kelp bed. Anyway, there'll be no living with these kids till they dig their fossils. And we can probably get a mess of clams for dinner. Suit you?"

Dick brought the dinghy back and rowed us ashore. Already the youngsters were halfway up the bank of cracked and weathered shale. There were tools enough to go around, so we all grabbed something and began digging in the crumbly bank. It's an eery, thrilling sensation to uncover shells several million years old; strange to realize that this perpendicular cliff once had been an ocean bottom before the buckling of the earth thrust it upright.

An hour later, hot, dirty, and tired, we gathered around Beth and her geology book. Very few of our "treasures" were whole; we had broken most of them getting them out. But by fitting the jigsaw pieces together, we could identify them by the descriptions and illustrations in the book.

"What's this thing?" Cookie asked. Beth thumbed through the pages and told him it must have been a baculite, a prehistoric great-grandfather of the chambered nautilus. We had segments of sea-going snails, forms of life unknown today. Even the cockleshells were slightly different than those around us on the beach. Mac had the prize, pieces of what appeared to be a petrified herring which still showed the sheen and opalescence of its scales.

We placed our fossils in the dinghy drawn up on the beach and we women crossed over a narrow spit of land to another bay. The men remained on Fossil Bay.

"We're in luck," Beth said, "no boats. We'll all have a good swim—raw." We still were undressing when we heard the men shout as they dived into the cold water; we could hear but not see them, for the neck of land between us was higher than the beach and covered with tall sawtooth grass. We waded into the water that was clear as jellyfish. It seemed colder without bathing suits, but after we ducked and got our breath, it was wonderful. Barbara's pigtails trailed out behind her as she dog-paddled to shore, leaving twin wakes behind them. Beth and I swam far out, reveling in the freedom of our bodies in that buoyant water. I felt as light and unencumbered as the spiked globes of dandelion fluff that bounced on the ripples beside us. Swimming back, I told Beth this must be heaven and I knew how angels felt, all spirit and no body. There was even a rosy little cherub on the beach.

"Who wants to hike over to Shallow Bay and dig clams?" Bill shouted to us as we dressed. We hurried and in no time were walking along a trail sweet with ferns and resin. It was cool here for the sun could not penetrate through the great shaggy branches of the firs. In the forest, breathing is like inhaling pure oxygen. Here was another beach, curved as the lip of a clam shell. We crossed a narrow isthmus to Shallow Bay and found the clam bed. The tide was well out, and all along the beach buried clams shot jets of water three or four inches into the air. Tiny brown crabs shuttled sideways under seaweed and, in a pool, sand dabs fluttered under the sand they so closely resembled. Gulls squawked and circled overhead.

Bill gathered the children around him, dug up a clam, and killed it with his knife. He cut one of the "hinges" on the shell so that its neck protruded limply. Then he said to the curious youngsters, "Now watch what happens. Gulls have bombsights. Just wait a moment." He tossed the clam quite a way down the beach. Soon a gull, cautious and stiff-legged, waddled toward it and grabbed the clam by the neck. The bird spiraled up and circled over a huge boulder, the clam dangling from its yellow beak. When he was directly over the rock, he dropped his prize. Seconds later, it smashed on the boulder and the gull darted after his dinner, butter-clam on the half-shell. Only there wasn't much shell left.

Mac dug a shallow hole near the water's edge and now the children were pawing around the rim of it, finding dozens of little white clams. They soon learned to distinguish the live clams from the heavier sand-filled "duds." After the pail was full, the boys begged to stay longer and collect some purple starfish that were wedged under the rocks exposed at low tide. But time and tide—and fishermen—wait for no one.

Back on the cruiser, we all snapped into action. Simultaneously, the gas stove was lighted, the anchor heaved up, and the engine started. As we headed out of the bay, the children were scrubbing the clams with sea water while I poured salad dressing over ten thousand vitamins. Soon the clams were steaming. They smelled like concentrated seashore. Bill looked up from the tackle he was rigging to sniff and rub his stomach. He said, "Steamed clams are my first love; garlic-butter bread, my second." He was licking his lips as he watched Beth shove a crunchy loaf in the oven.

"Where do I come in?" I inquired.

"Right after the garlic bread, dear. You and a forty-five-pound king tie for third place. Say, where's my fishing hat? I took it off when I went ashore."

"*Your* hat? What d'you mean? It's still open season." I looked around and didn't see it, so I said, "There's a pile of dust in that corner. Perhaps that's the remains of the hat. Maybe it fell to pieces—like the One-Horse Shay."

But it hadn't. Bill yipped happily as he unearthed it behind a cushion. Lovingly he punched it into a resemblance of shape and slapped it on his head, saying, "How about it? Want to settle this thing once and for all tonight? Tomorrow, it will be either your hat or mine. Okay?"

"Fine with me," I answered absently, my head in a billow of steam. "Round up the crew. These clams are done." I lifted them from the big kettle and strained the nectar through a cloth to catch the sand. Then I poured this delicious clam broth into cups, added a dash of tabasco sauce and a floater of butter. The clams went back into the pail and Bill carried it to the cockpit. Mac, at the wheel, had his dinner in what we referred to as "solitary refinement" while the rest of us sat on the deck, circled around the bucket of clams. From that moment on until it was empty, somebody's hand was always dipping into it.

"Careful of the sand, children," Beth warned. "Clams really should stand in salt water overnight and then they would clean themselves. So watch out. Try rinsing each one in the nectar first and then remember, don't quite drain your cup. Aren't they wonderful?"

Beside the great mounds of tossed salad on our plates, we each had a paper cup of melted butter, and soon even the children had a perfect chain-stroke rhythm: shells were opened with fingers, clams pried out with forks, swished in nectar, then in melted butter, and popped into mouths. Only Barbara didn't like them. She complained that she didn't want to eat *anybody's* stomach. Bill said that a Kansas City sirloin wouldn't have tasted so good. The well-named nectar tasted as though all the goodness and tang of the sea had been distilled into it. The last shell was thrown overboard as Mac cut the engine to trolling speed. We were off the kelp bed.

Soon three lines were in the water, a rod out either side of the boat, and one straight back off the stern. With so many of us aboard, we legally could have had eight lines in use, but unless a boat is especially rigged for commercial fishing with long arms at the sides, three is the most that may be let out with comfort. At that, one must be careful not to allow the lines to tangle when the boat turns sharply. In small boats with outboard motors, fussy fishermen often will not permit a third line. And anybody in any sized craft that gets his line fouled around the propeller may expect to be shunned for years to come.

Mac wouldn't relinquish the wheel, insisting that Bill fish, as he had already landed one big king. He lit his pipe and settled down on the high stool to go round and round the kelp bed. He gave us peace and quiet by telling the children grim stories about how the unwarlike San Juan Indians were massacred by the northern tribes. Blood fairly dripped off each verb. He certainly knew how to hold his audience. Mentally, I was assigning him to the nightmare watch.

On deck, it was getting cold. Heavy coats felt good as we relaxed in the canvas chairs. The calm water was taking on a deep indigo blue. There was a mile-wide copper path leading toward the sunset. I was just thinking that the mountains needed to be three shades darker for hot fishing when Beth had a strike. The rod lurched in her hands as the line whipped out. Surprised, she yelled and almost dropped it. Beth had spent more time being a lady than a fishwife, so now she turned startled blue eyes on Bill.

"Good work, Beth. Hang on tight and reel in," he said gallantly, bringing in his own line. I was pulling in, too—and illogically nursing a bit of feminine resentment. What do blue eyes have that brown eyes don't? That round, wide kind. If I'd fumbled my rod, Bill would have called me a clumsy baboon.

"Look. It's gone!" she whimpered, bringing in a slack line.

"Maybe not. Perhaps he's just coming toward the boat," Bill said soothingly.

But the salmon was gone. Beth reeled in and the slip sinker already had gone down the line. She lifted in the red-headed plug; all the hooks had been torn off. That fish had left only a frayed end of white cord as a calling card.

"Must have been a big fella," Bill said sympathetically as he chose another plug from Mac's box, this time a Lucky Louie with drop hooks on a chain. Smiling like Sir Galahad, he showed her how to twist it on a new leader, and he told her the way to hang onto pet plugs was to put on a new leader after each fish.

After he had finished, he tossed it overside, tested the action, and he must have liked it for he let the line out. He handed the rod back to her. The herring on my hooks looked bedraggled, so my husband told me to put on another. Bill and I were using some of Cappy Bell's herring which had been kept on ice, so this meant limbering the beast up; it was so thoroughly dead and stiff that it had to be worked and twisted if it were to flutter in the water.

When I finally had the lead hook through its mouth and the two gang hooks on either side, I tried its action in the water. Bill peered over my shoulder and said, "Atta girl." I was only partially mollified; my hands smelled so of herring that I would gladly have ex-

changed a pound of pride for an ounce of chivalry.
Right then I decided the smartest women are blonde,
willing and as incapable as possible.

We fished for quite a while. A little wind came up
and Bill, pulling his neck down further in his coat, murmured something I didn't understand about taking the
brass monkeys in tonight. I didn't think I'd ever learn
all the fishing terms. Once when Mac was making a
wide turn around the head of the kelp bed, both Bill
and I tied into a couple of dogfish. He cut them off the
hooks and threw them back before rebaiting.

Then Beth got her gear hooked up on kelp, though
she honestly couldn't be blamed too much for she was
fishing next to it. Bill and I reeled in and he took her
rod, thrashing it up and down and sideways as he tried
to work the hooks out of that tough, fibrous tube. Mac
reversed the engine and, right over the spot, Bill tugged
and yanked but he might as well have tried to lift the
ocean floor. Often hooks can be dislodged by backing
over the place where they are caught and pulling in the
opposite direction. But it was no go this time. He leaned
far over the transom. Red-faced and exasperated, he
gave a particularly hard pull on the line itself. It snapped
just below the surface and loosely whipped back in his
face.

It was a bit forced, but he still smiled at Beth as he
took a new plug from its box and twisted it on a new
leader wire. Standing up, he grasped Beth's rod, and
tossed the plug overside.

"We'll test its action," he said.

I looked at it in the water and said bitingly, "You
mean it'll test *yours*." For the plug was bouncing in the

wake of the boat, trailing behind it the leader wire Bill had forgotten to attach to the cuttyhunk line.

"Hey! Mac . . . reverse. Beth, hand me that net." His tone was no longer courtly. And now I smiled. It took some time to locate the plug in the churning water, but he finally did and scooped it up in the net.

Again lines were out and expectancy sharpened our wits. Bill was in an expansive mood.

"Funny thing about fishing," he said, "the way it shows up a man's hidden traits."

"What d'you mean?" I asked, suspiciously. But I relaxed as he continued.

"Oh, just what I said. You can learn more about a man in a given length of time on a fishing trip than any other way. It doesn't take long to get him pegged.

"For instance, there's the poor sport who cusses and bangs the outboard motor when it balks, finds fault with the tackle, and sulks when the fish don't bite. If he's your guest, using your boat and gear, he's the meanie who grabs all the fish for himself if he does catch any without even offering to divide them. He doesn't know it, but that's his last trip with you.

"Then there's the blow-hard who never caught a fish all by himself, but when he does land one on your tackle and with your guiding, he gloats all over the place. Invariably, he spends the rest of the trip explaining *his* theories on fishing and how good he is. At this point the blow-hard takes a drink and soon becomes insufferable in his I'll-buy-Alaska-if-you-wish-to-sell mood. He'll tell you all about the *great big ones* he took out of Butterfly Creek when he was a boy back in Nebraska. He's sure to be the guy who can't bait his own hook and manages to be fiddling around in the boat when it's time to clean the fish. Later, when you're unloading the tackle and gas cans and motor, he's still telling you how to fish—from a log on the beach."

Bill grunted at these memories and cleaned grass off his setup before continuing this one-way conversation.

He said, "Deliver me from the eager beaver who *must* have fish to prove his manhood. That dope's out for meat, not sport. He cries in his beer if he doesn't get any and ends up by complaining that it's a lousy old man's game anyway. He's a headache.

"But, you know, most fishermen are good sports. And the better fishermen, the better sports. Remember, Bea, I told you about that trip with Elmer Satterberg? How he helped with the motor, cut the spinners, and insisted we take his fish because we had a canning spree on. I wouldn't take all of them, but I appreciated the offer.

"Yep, fishing's a good way to judge a man. I read about a famous French woman of letters who claimed no woman should marry a man until she had seen him in his cups—that this was a sure-fire way to see his inner self. Well, there's some sense to her idea but, if she'd ever been fishing, she would have known a better plan."

After the oracle had spoken, Beth and I nodded flatteringly and turned our attention to the gulls that swooped down toward the floating streamers of kelp where the herring "boiled." Occasionally they must have burped, for tiny bubbles wavered up to the surface. They certainly weren't king-sized belches. Bill shoved his fishing hat back on his head and waved in the direction of the sunset-stained Canadian mountains, saying, "That's the right color. Any time, now. This outgoing tide should sweep a lot of Orcas Island fish over here. They should follow the back eddy into this pool and—"

"Say," I interrupted, "with all that knowledge inside your head, you don't need that magic hat on top of it. Give it to me. Besides, if you remember, you haven't any more right to wear it than I have. Gimme."

As I put it on, my rod jumped and the tip flew down in a sharp curve. The line whizzed out.

"Kelp?" Beth asked—a trifle hopefully, I thought.

"Not on your life! Fish on, Mac," I yelled. Instantly he threw the gear into neutral.

"Acts like a big ling cod." Beth wasn't going to give up easily.

"Cod!" I snorted, for the rod was pounding in my hands as the salmon jerked off yards with each short, frantic run. No loggy proletarian cod ever had this much spunk. That salmon was kicking up its heels and I shot Beth a triumphant glance. Who was envying who now? I was on my own stamping grounds—bring on your big blue eyes.

Now the line was veering toward the kelp bed. "Watch out!" Bill was yelling like a Siwash Indian on a Saturday-night spree. "If it gets in that stuff, all hell will break loose." As there is no known way to stop a husband from giving advice, I ignored it. But I did lift my rod high so this water buffalo would have more to pull against. Then Bill told me to start pumping him in but, just as I got set, that salmon tore through the water toward Mount Baker as though he were getting a running jump and going to scale it.

Feet apart and braced, I hung onto that rod that was pounding as hard as my heart. More line ripped out with fierce, angry yanks. It hadn't jumped so I knew it was a king. He was mad at me and the battle was on. I was in my element—but so was he. Given a little slack,

it would be no trick at all for that moose to throw a
fatal kink in the stiff wire leader. Now the rod was just
wavering in slow, steady curves as though it were tired,
and the line snorted out only a few feet at a time. I
pumped it in, but that fish fought every inch I wound
on the reel. If there hadn't been that constant quiver, it
might have been a sack of cement on the line. I was
tired—achingly tired.

"Tell me, Bill," I panted, "how do you get more snap
in your synapsis?"

"You better worry about the snap in your rod. Look
at it, not me." I had let it droop almost horizontally, so
I hoisted it up again, luckily, as the king changed his
mind. He tore out like a scared wolf, but I was ready
for him when he quit. Bill thumped me on the back,
saying, "Swell going. Wish Cappy could see you now.
You're sure 'learnin'.'"

"Still learning? Nuts. This is graduate work," I
grunted, fighting a line taut as a fiddle string.

"Okay. But you don't get a diploma till he's in the
boat."

My wrists were throbbing with a killing weariness; I
reeled in more slowly. All of us were peering down into
the water when the slip sinker came into view. That
first tug had sent it flying down the line to the leader.
I lifted the rod and the silvery wire inched out of the
water. Then we saw him. What a salmon! It was well
over a yard long and its rounded greenish back looked
six inches across.

"Get its head up. Lift him a little more. But easy."
Now Bill was excited. Praying those triple hooks would
hold, I pulled up on the rod a trifle more.

"That's it. Hand me the gaff. Look at that head and

jaw. He's got a mighty mean expression," Bill said, ready to gaff him.

Then that king quivered in wrath, jerked a foot off the reel, and flailing the surface with his broad tail, shot down. As it ran out, I glared at Bill. He had done it. I remembered Hannah's words: "Personal remarks are always odious."

But the line flowed out smoothly. This was a quiet, spent run, very different from his first desperate stampede. The rod hardly vibrated as the cuttyhunk poured out and I imagined this last stately run to be a king's farewell to his domain. Then he stopped and came willingly toward the boat as though it were beneath his dignity to struggle when he knew that he must abdicate.

He surfaced and rolled drunkenly. Now Bill was poised above him with the gaff hook. There was a quick, sure, upward pull and the hook slipped under a gill cover. Straining, he heaved the king over the gunwale and dropped it on the deck. As it hit, the one remaining hook in its mouth fell out.

"Gosh," Beth breathed, stepping back out of the way of its thrashing tail. "He must be old enough to vote!" Solemnly, Bill handed *me* the lead pipe. Quivering from fatigue and cold chills, I knocked it hard on the head. I still was panting when I straightened up. During the fray, the fishing hat had fallen off and now Bill picked it up. With all the pomp of a knighting ceremony, he bowed low before placing it on my head. "It's yours, my dear. Won fair and aboveboard. I'll never beat that tonight—it must run thirty pounds. Good going. I'm proud of you."

I took the wheel as it was Mac's turn to fish now. Sitting down on that comfortably padded stool felt good. Alone, I could indulge in a fatuous smile all I wanted to while I told the children about the big one that *didn't* get away. But they quickly tired of my heroics, so I steered around the kelp bed with one hand and unfastened buttons with the other. Soon they were asleep in their bunks.

Feeling very silly and thoroughly enjoying it, I propped a mirror in front of me and tried flipping the brim of my hat at different angles. Unfortunately, I didn't need the mirror to know I had that hat on, and I wondered if some high-powered sachet under the sweat band would help. I took it off and looked at it critically. A royal coachman fell from the tattered ribbon. If I put on a fresh band, would that break the magic? Probably would. Better not monkey with it. Bet Lilly Daché never turned out a more promising hat and . . .

"Hey! What you doing in there?" Bill was hollering at me as only a husband may. "Look where you're heading!"

I did—and spun the wheel hard to starboard. We were almost on the kelp and I began praying no one would get his gear hung up on that stuff. It was a long prayer, for it took a couple of minutes to be sure the lines trailing eighty feet behind the cruiser had safely missed it.

Alert now, I strained to see, watching for any stragglers floating out from the main bed. But it was hard to keep my eyes glued on that rose-tinted water. The evening itself was enough of a distraction, for the sunset was spilling a skyful of gold over the mountains. Silver edges do a lot for even a pink cloud. The west was aflame. Suddenly, dozens of delicate, long-legged snipes flitted to a stop and rested on the kelp. As they preened their feathers with long bills, they looked like little six-inch storks. Or as real storks might have appeared viewed through the wrong end of binoculars. Then, as if from some signal, they all whirred into the air at once and darted past like bits of tissue paper in a gale. I watched their lightning flight until they were lost in the distance. And then I drew a breath.

We were trolling right over that pool I had picked out on the chart when Bill yelled to cut the motor. I could hear Beth and Mac reel in as Bill's line screeched.

"Big one?" I called. I couldn't leave the wheel, for we were very near the kelp and if we drifted too close, I'd have to start up again. No one answered. Later, Bill shouted, "Just a cod." There was a liar's note in his voice, but complacency dulled my wits and I believed him. During the fight, I had to ease into low speed several times to keep off the kelp. I was so busy I didn't notice how long it took Bill to bring in that fish—too long to horse in a lumbering cod. I heard them shout as Mac gaffed it. There were oddly exuberant yells as it hit the deck. Something was wrong here.

Very soon Bill sauntered in the cabin and, hands on hips, smiled down at me. But his eyes were on my hat.

"Too bad," he said suavely. "On you it looks good."

"What do you mean?" I was half afraid I knew.

"I mean, darling, that your hat is about to revert to its rightful owner."

"Not for a thousand-pound cod! You know we never count those belly-crawling things." I jammed the hat more firmly on my head. But with maddening deliberation he leaned against the cabin door, folded his arms, and smirked at me.

"Yours is a good fish—for a woman. C'mon out on deck and see what a man can do." Now my doubts had balled up into indignation. I yelled to Beth to come in and take the wheel. I followed Bill outside and stopped in my tracks. There, stretched out side by side, were two great kings.

"Twins?" I asked hopefully. They looked the same size.

"Are you blind?" Bill roared. "Can't you see my fish is a good inch longer than yours?" It was true. Mac was sitting on the rail and laughing at us.

"Hate to do it," Bill said, each oily word slipping over the other. He was reaching for my hat when Mac broke in: "Hold on a minute. Salmon are judged by poundage, not length. Maybe the lady still wins. Wait till I get the scales."

He dove into the cabin and returned with spring scales. He held them up while Bill slipped his fish on. By flashlight, we watched the needle quiver to a stop on the twenty-nine-pound mark.

"Still want to weigh that minnow of yours?"

I held it up myself and put it on the hook, hardly breathing while the pointer quieted down. It was smack on the thirty-pound line. "Hey," Bill yelled, "I don't believe it."

But it was true—my king was a pound heavier than his. He just gaped at the scales, saying slowly, "Well, I'm a . . ."

"Yes, you are," I agreed happily, fingering my hat. Now both salmon were on the deck and Bill, stooped over them, was giving out with war talk. He was measuring the girths of the kings with a piece of leader wire.

"Bust and hips practically the same," he said, "though I think mine's a trifle bigger around. And it's certainly longer. I . . . don't . . . understand," he murmured. He still was jabbering to himself when Mac took the wheel and headed back toward Fossil Bay. It was dark now and fishing was over.

A few hundred feet off shore, Mac cut the motor and a wonderful soft black silence settled around us. On deck Bill was tossing the kings into the dinghy while Mac let out the anchor. I was busy, too, watching the Great Dipper scoop up the tips of fir trees. Bill was already in the dinghy when Mac came aft, carrying a lantern.

He said, "Wait till I light it. You can't clean fish in the dark." It was a gasoline Coleman lantern. Beth and I hid our heads as he pumped up the lethal thing. When he lit it, there was a brilliant, whitish light and it hissed like seven devils. Mac handed it down to Bill, saying, "Cut the stomachs open. Let's see what those kings are feeding on."

Beth started for bed, but I was perfectly willing to sit on deck and listen to the quiet. Looking down into the water, I could see the phosphorescent glow of tiny fish as they swept past and I knew those round blobs of light were the undulating jellyfish—ghosts of the sea outlined in this weird, greenish luminescence. A bit of star-spangled driftwood floated past. Sparks struck from its edges. A school of candlefish were just a gleam as they shot through the water.

I could see Bill ashore. He had just put out the lantern. Now he was rowing back with unusually quick, decisive strokes. With every thrust, the bow struck phosphorus sparks and there were pools of light wherever he dipped his oars.

As the dinghy came alongside, Mac returned to deck

and switched on the mast light. He seemed to be vastly amused over something as he grabbed the salmon Bill was hoisting up to him.

"What were they feeding on, Bill? Big herring?"

"*Mine* was," he said ominously. He climbed aboard and faced Mac. "But, you double-dyed devil, Bea's king had three lead sinkers down its throat. Must have swallowed three setups and digested the hooks and leaders. Only the leads were left." Grinning, Bill poked Mac hard in the ribs, adding, "You don't happen to know anything about it, do you?"

Bill handed Mac the scales, saying, "I demand a recount. Any guy low enough to load fish would trample on young corn. Steady now."

I watched them weigh in both fish again, feeling as though I had a dozen lead sinkers in *my* stomach. My salmon, after it had been cleaned—and the lead removed —weighed a little over twenty-five pounds. Bill let it flop to the deck and put his on the scales.

"Read it and weep," he yowled. The needle almost reached twenty-six pounds. While he was telling me that mine was a ripe female and must have almost a pound of eggs in her, I was reconstructing the crime. Mac had had plenty of time to load my king while Bill had been in the cabin boasting to me.

I shook off a slight touch of rigor mortis, handed Bill my hat, and gulped, "Okay, Big Wheel. It's yours. I'm going in the cabin and make some coffee. I need it."

"Me, too," Bill said happily.

"Will you make me a cup?" Mac asked sheepishly.

"No. I'm going to mix a Socrates highball for you."

"What's that?"

"Plain water—and two jiggers of Old Hemlock."

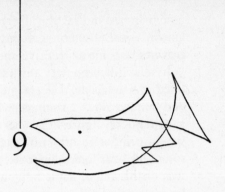

9

Opening day is a double-header

For the next few years, I couldn't catch time by the dorsal fin as it swam by. The boys progressed from "Cops-and-robbers," through marbles to sand-lot football. Their new fishing rods were two feet longer. They skied instead of roller-skated, and in place of lizards, brought home cunning little girls. I braced myself for the emotional upheaval of early adolescence. I was prepared for anything—except what happened.

It's no trick at all to meet a natural and expected phenomenon head on and take it in your stride. But an *unnatural* one is highly disturbing and we had a beauty at our house. For it was the boys' *father* who went

mooning around with all the adolescent symptoms.
Cookie and Bob were perfectly normal, a nice set of ex-
troverts bursting with drive and enthusiasm.

It was Bill who was restless and dreamy, yet every
once in a while he'd get a gleam in his eye. It was all
very mysterious. Evenings, when he wasn't adding up
a column of figures that he wouldn't let me see, he
would grin, stare off into space, and then dash upstairs
to use his bedroom telephone. He wouldn't tell us what
was on his mind; something was up. This couldn't all
be spring fever.

For an Easter present, the boys gave him two joined
spools of Monel metal fishing line which he took with
him on a "men only" trip to Orcas. He returned with
no fish—and no improvement in his general symptoms.
He was evasive when we plied him with questions and,
for the first time in his life, he was disinterested in fishing. Totally preoccupied, he told us nothing. Bob whispered he had not even unwound the new line onto his
reel.

One evening in April, I listened for storm warnings
as Bill drove into the garage. I sighed when I heard the
car door slam. Hard. I tried to tell myself that he was
just concerned about a patient, that somebody was going to lose some plumbing or maybe an appendix. I
asked him when he came in and flopped down in his
chair. But it wasn't that. I tried all the prescribed
wifely wiles, hinting about roast beef and apple pie for
dinner. It didn't interest him. This was bad because
food *always* interested Bill. Even when he was sick in
bed himself during a "flu" epidemic, he consumed
mounds of roast pork and mince pie while advising pa-

tients similarly affected to eat "a little thin toast, a little weak gruel, and tea."

Now he fished around in his pockets and extracted a lot of small packages which he tossed onto the davenport. Uncle Walter, our new black tomcat, began batting them around. Wordlessly, Bill reached for the *Seattle Times* and snapped it open. The way he rustled his newspaper was a sure index of his mood. Tonight it crackled like a bush fire.

"What's the matter, Bill? Can't you tell me?"

"Oh—something's cooking. I'll tell you soon. Not now."

At that moment, Cookie and Bob tore through the room, leaving a wake of baseball bats and shin guards behind them. Radiant and grimy, they headed for the lavatory. As a forced concession to respectability, they wet their hands and faces, wiped them reasonably clean on towels, and combed the hair immediately above their foreheads until it was slick as a seal. The bristling back hair was untouched and looked as though it had been whipped with an egg beater.

At dinner my husband said, almost incidentally, "How'd you like to go to Orcas Island this Saturday? Hit Cascade Lake on the opening day. Want to?" There was none of the usual Orcas fire in his voice. As the boys leaped up and rushed to his side, one chair was tipped over, Uncle Walter yowled as he was stepped on, and Bonnie began to bark.

"Mean it, Dad? Us, too?"

"Yep. It's a promise. Should be a good trip—I hope." As Cookie thwacked him excitedly on the back, Bill brightened a little and added, "I brought home some new tackle. We'll get it lined up and varnish our rods tonight."

I hadn't said a word and now he looked at me curiously, saying, "What's the matter, Bea? Don't you want to go?"

With effort, I pulled myself together. "Of course. It'll be great fun." But my voice sounded hollow even to myself.

By four-thirty Saturday afternoon, we were in Anacortes, lined up for the six o'clock ferry. There would be a jam-packed load of cars tonight, for the opening of the trout season tomorrow in Cascade Lake would be a gala event, drawing well over one hundred fishermen from the mainland. Men in plaid shirts and canvas pants were piling in and out of the waiting cars and calling to each other with that contagious optimism of fishermen. Friends who might see each other only once a year, at this time, were slapping each other on the back. There was a thrill and tingle in the air and the excitement got under my skin.

Finally the big ferry plowed in and, after discharging its load from the Islands, tooted twice and we drove aboard. We found Cookie and Bob in the main salon— if you care to call it that—for they had dashed on ahead of us to save seats at the lunch counter. They had saved them, all right. With men lined up and waiting behind each stool, we noticed four unexplainable vacancies. Then Cookie and Bob found us in the crowd and handed us the heads of the stools which they had removed from the shafts. Embarrassed, we fitted them on and ordered quickly.

It was he-man food, good, but guaranteed to grow

hair on the chest. After a full course dinner, including fried potatoes and pork chops, it took a chocolate malted milk to satisfy the boys.

"Dad," Bob spoke with a foamy gargle as he put the empty glass on the counter, "is it harder to get silver or rainbow trout?"

"Well, I'll tell you. Rainbows hang around the bottom of the lake and that makes it harder to judge where they are. You don't very often get them trolling so we're going to still-fish—with preserved salmon eggs. Jess White gave me some good dope and warned me to beat the crowd to his favorite hole. I know where it is, too, but we'll have to get up early."

I winced, thinking if all the mornings I'd gotten up at four in the morning were laid end to end. . . .

Bill was happily chatting with fishermen he knew, so the boys and I went out to the afterdeck. We marveled at the way the ferry twisted between the Islands, through passes that would break a snake's back.

The hour-and-a-half trip was over too soon; just ahead were the twinkling lights of that tiny little town called Orcas. As the ferry ground her snout against the pilings, we hurried into the car. Bill swears his blood pressure drops twenty points after the ferry docks and we enter "our other world" where peace rolls in with the tide and people have time for kindness.

We drove through the sweet-smelling night to the village of East Sound. There, Templin's Store was a blaze of lights and we had trouble finding a place to park our car. It looked interesting and I was glad we had to drop in here to buy our fishing licenses. Cookie and Bob, being under sixteen, didn't need them.

We pushed our way into the rambling one-story

building which has changed little in fifty years. Judg-
ing from the crowd of people milling about, half the
fishermen on the island were here. Soon Bill spotted
Karl Templin, who is master of ceremonies at this fam-
ily-run store.

"Glad to see you're going after 'em, Bill," Karl said,
looking at us over his glasses. I like this pert, wiry man
who is quite a bit on the far side of middle age. After
we had chatted about crops and fishing in general, I
asked Karl if he thought it would rain tomorrow.

"It may—and what if it does? Let me tell you, a rainy
day on Orcas Island is a sight better than a sunny one
in the city. You know," he said, his face wrinkling into
a dry smile, "recently I spent six weeks in Seattle—all
in one afternoon." He started to make out our licenses
but was interrupted constantly by fishermen who asked
him for advice. He was a local fount of wisdom and so
at home on Orcas that I suspected he was here when the
glaciers receded and the island was built around him.

This fascinating country store was the social center
of the island; it took the place of clubs and pubs. The
boys and I wandered around, delighted with the sights
and smells. In a side room, fishermen were seated on
kegs of nails near the pot-bellied stove. It hissed in re-
taliation at the scatter-shot of the starched-pants Sunday
fishermen whose aim fell short of the spittoon beyond.
Old-timers had no trouble. There was a furious poker
game in progress, and at regular intervals the players
dipped into the huge bowl of hoarhound candy on the
counter. Bill had told me this free candy was a courtesy
of the house, put out in October and removed in May
before the city slickers came to eat it all up. It was a
real poker game and the stakes were high, along with

numerous side bets as to who'd get the most rainbows in the morning.

The smoke-filled air, gray as evening mist, was a blend of fifty-cent Coronas and evil-smelling "Rum-Soaked Crooks" which resembled bent sticks of licorice candy. There were overtones of kerosene, coffee in the grinder, rubber boots, and horse linament. The rafters overhead were hung with milking pails, harness, rope, feed bags, and almost everything else farmers or fishermen could want. On one wall was a placard announcing the big Fishermen's Ball that was being held that night.

We returned to the main room where Karl was cutting great slabs of cheese, no doubt for early morning sandwiches. He and Bill were still talking about fishing; my husband was pumping him for all those little trout tricks he knew.

I pulled Bill away, for that dawn hour would come very soon, and we headed for our cabin. Bill said we were getting up at three o'clock.

"Three!"

"That's right. We have to beat a lot of boats to that favorite hole. Now you all turn in. I have a long-distance phone call to make."

He gave no further explanation, and thinking discretion the better part of valor, I didn't ask the questions teeming in my mind. The boys were asleep before I was—long before.

"Up and at 'em," Bill was chanting, insufferably cheerful. The glare from a naked electric light bulb searched under my eyes and I looked around. The windows were squares of black, the rafters lost in darkness. Clothes were strewn over the too-early American furniture. Bill, trying to light the cook stove, was no

Romeo in his long wool underwear. But I wasn't any Juliet myself as I dragged out of bed and yanked too-snug jeans on over my own trap-door specials.

"These darned pants get smaller every year," I groused. "They just don't fit."

Bill looked me over appraisingly, fore and aft, and then said, "Where don't they fit?"

This remark didn't help my feelings any but, later, coffee did. A farm-hand breakfast fixed the men up in no time; the boys were so bright-eyed and bushy-tailed, their exuberance wore me out. Anyway, I was cross about missing the fancy Fishermen's Breakfast at the inn. Why did we always have to be a full hour ahead of the herd? At that, Bill made us fairly throw the food down our faces, he was in such a fever to get started. I struggled into my sheepskin coat and raced for the car, hoping the rainbows would appreciate all my efforts.

At the lake, we parked in a grove of huge cedars, Bill muttering about the few cars ahead of us. I teased Bill, reminding him that early birds got worms and how would he like that? He just grunted and led the way by flashlight to the boat dock. There, hundreds of rowboats, trucked in from all over the island and many from the mainland, were waiting and ready. The park attendant indicated our reserved boat, saying, "Good thing I'm here early. But I knew there'd be a few damfools like you." After we had piled in with our rods and creels, he shoved us off with a warning: "The game warden doesn't care if you sit out there all night. But remember, don't wet a line until dawn."

Bill rowed and it was like pushing through a black velvet curtain. By four-fifteen we were at the other end of the lake which is about three-fourths of a mile in length. Bill jockeyed around quite awhile before he sensed the place to drop the two stones which served as prow and stern anchors. I could hardly see a thing, but he swore we were lined up with a certain shadowy tree on one bank and a dock on the other.

"Watch 'em head this way," he crowed. "We've beat the crowd. I fished it once with Jess White. He's a linguist, speaks three languages—English, Salmon, and Trout. Watch the time, Cookie."

The sky was becoming tattle-tale gray, and the stars which had looked so virile now were anemic. It was shivering cold and a wind sprang up which poked icy fingers down my neck. But Bill loved it, explaining how a ripple on the surface makes fishing better as it distorts the reflection of the line.

"It's quarter to five now, Dad," Cookie said, yawning. He pinched his brother, hoping for a little excitement. He got it. Inactivity was not his dish. By flashlight, Bill was setting up the rods. He glanced around to check the landmarks.

" 'Bout right. We ought to be over the hole. You see, now we will be fishing where there's a sand and gravel bottom instead of a place choked with weeds."

He was unwinding a thread-thin leader that was seven feet long; it was one-pound-test and had a tiny size twelve hook attached.

"I like the silver hooks best. Always imagine I can see the shadow of a gold hook through the egg. If I can, Lord knows a trout can, too." About three feet back from the hook, he clamped on a split-shot sinker; it looked like a small bead cut halfway through its diameter.

"That holds the line down on bottom and lets the

rest of the leader swing free. For rainbows in this lake, the eggs have to be on bottom." He bit the bead sinker together with his teeth.

"Don't do that," I exploded. "You'll crack the enamel!"

He bit it again before he answered, unperturbed, "That's okay. You don't need teeth to fish. Some of the best fishermen I know don't have any at all." He tied the webby leaders to the oiled silk lines on all four rods, laid them carefully lengthwise of the boat, and then pulled a small stone from his pocket. He tied a piece of string crisscross around it.

"Now, everybody gets a turn with this stone. Slip your hook through the string, put it overside, and let out line till it hits bottom." When Bob had done so, Bill tied a bit of red thread on the line about three feet back from the tip of the rod.

"When you are fishing, let out line until this thread is at the tip of your rod. That will mean your sinker is on bottom with three feet of leader swinging free."

While we were marking our lines, he told us that silver trout are not fussy for they take bait eight or ten inches off bottom. We were so absorbed we did not notice the boats clustering around us. But we did hear old cronies calling back and forth to each other. Hunched down in their coats, they were dark silhouettes against the gun-metal water.

"Hey, Dad. It's five minutes of five," Cookie said, impatiently. "Do we have to wait seven whole minutes?"

His father answered, "I've waited all winter for this. Seven more minutes won't bother me. Look at the boats down there by the bridge."

"Is this the best hole on the lake?" Bob asked.

"Jess says it is, but I know of several other good places. There's one near the road off a half-sunken log, and a lot of men swear that it's hot near the outlet."

Now that there was only a minute or two left before official sunrise, everybody was anxiously fingering his line and yelling to neighboring boats.

"Hi, there! Isn't that Bill Cook?" Bill squinted in the half light and grinned.

"Hi, yourself, Deskin. Who's that old trout grabber with you, Ben Paris?" Bill pointed out other friends: Wes Langell, Howard Porter, and young Chuck Gerard. Opening day was old home week.

"It's five right this minute. C'mon, let's start," Cookie urged, dangling his line in the water. "Look, those guys have."

"Mebbe their watches are wrong," Bill answered, winking. "We'll wait two minutes and make it legal. Here's some gum. Take your energy out on that."

Now a gray veil was lifting from the world and trees were outlined against the sky, and the shining, golden beauty of the morning loosened all the knots in my nerves. This lovely fir-trimmed lake nestled between Mount Entrance and Tommy High, an underprivileged mountain but rounded and beautiful.

"Okay! It's okay now, everybody!" Cookie's shout was lost in the backwash of cheering that floated up the lake. With whistles and yells, hundreds of lines plopped in at once. But Bill had waited for better light to bait the hooks. Now the boat rocked dangerously as we gathered around to watch him. From a jar of reddish-orange salmon eggs, he picked a nice one and said, "You have to be democratic. I've known some one-egg men who were just as good as any two-egg man you ever saw. But I like two eggs myself." He worked the first egg well up on the hook so that it completely covered the shaft. Then he took another and, with a circular sort of twist, curled the hook through it until just the point protruded through the tough skin of the egg.

The boys and I had our lines in when we noticed Bill's rod still beside him. Of all things, he was fiddling with a tiny slingshot! Wondering if he had slipped a cog, I saw him scoop tiny red feed eggs from another jar, place them in the leather pad, and pull back on the elastic bands. When he let go, the eggs shot far out into the water. Pleased as any ten-year-old, he said, "See? Those eggs will draw the trout from all around here. Pretty soon I'll shoot again, only not quite so far. It will lead them in closer. After that, I can just toss the eggs in. Not too many, just enough to whet their appetites." He shot a few all around the boat and said, "It's a swell theory. Let's see if it works. Here's another point. Occasionally, move your bait just a trifle. It might be hidden by a bit of weed or something. Karl Templin gave me that tip last night."

I was relieved when he dropped his line in—and put the slingshot away. That thing and the silly grin he wore when he used it smacked too much of delayed adolescence. Now somebody near us yelled "first fish" as he landed a beauty. Jealous eyes pivoted in his direction. This inspiration was all we needed to concentrate on our own lines. Most of the fishermen in boats were quiet, except one where two men were standing up and wavering around. They were more interested in a flat bottle than their lines. Singing "Little Brown Jug," the men were betting each other the Empire State building that they would catch "more damn fish than anybody in the w-o-r-l-d." Bill eyed them disapprovingly and said, "I'll lay you even money that one of those idiots falls in." The boys were gaping at them.

"Say, fellas, you better watch your rods instead. You have to be on the job. When you see the line begin to straighten out, that's the second to give him a quick, snappy little jerk."

"Him?" Cookie twinkled. " 'Spose it's a 'her'? Then do you jerk it just as hard?"

"Naw, you don't have to. Females bite on anything and hang on." Bill grinned and was waiting to get a rise out of me when Bob hollered and whipped his rod so high that it arched back over his shoulder.

"Strike?" Bill asked.

"Thought so," Bob said, reeling in until he could lift the leader out of the water.

"Well, if you did have one, either you beat him to the draw or wrenched the hook out of his mouth. Let's see it." Sure enough, there were threads of cartilage clinging to the barb. Bob looked at it ruefully, sniffed, wiped his nose on the back of his hand, started to defend himself, and then thought better of it.

"Don't get so excited next time." Bill inspected his own bait before continuing. "Setting a hook is like doing lots of other things, son. It isn't the heft you use but the finesse. Muscle doesn't mean a thing—it's good timing that counts. 'Know-how' turns the trick every time. It's true in lots of other situations, too. Remember that."

We had plenty of time to dwell on this Golden Text, for our lines just soaked while everybody around us killed fish. The trollers were rowing, slowly sneaking in

close to sunken logs and other fishy habitats. One of
the two dozen or so trollers near us suddenly shipped
his oars with a clatter and grabbed the rod that was lying
in the boat with the line straight back over the stern. He
reeled in and soon we could see the glittering pop gear
whirl through the water as he netted a nice silver trout.
I didn't envy him rebaiting as he was having a terrible
time working that wriggling worm over the point of the
hook. It would slither out of his fingers and fall under
the floorboards. Then he'd choose another from the
earth-filled coffee can, stirring up the soil with an irri-
tated finger. With a new and fatter worm, he tried
again and I knew how that slimy thing was thinning
out when it felt the hook. Finally, in exasperation, he
yelled at it, "Aw buck up, fella. Lemme stick this hook
in yuh."

My attention snapped back to Bob who was making
a series of peculiar guttural noises, and I saw him jerk
his rod up—just a few inches. Instantly the line spun
out and we reeled in to give him the field. He needed
it. His trout was jitterbugging all over the place. Now
the line was cutting its rippling V toward a snag some
thirty feet away.

"Tell him 'No.'" Cookie shouted advice, and I
thought the taint must be in his blood. Both lads were
moving around in the boat and it rocked precariously.
I slipped out of my bulky sheepskin coat—just in case.

"*You* tell him 'No.' I'm busy," Bob panted. He was,
too. Coached by his father, he lifted his rod high, just
in time to slow that mad dash. Then, the unexpected
lightning flashback. But, reeling hard, Bob picked up the
slack in time. Now I could see a glint of color as the
trout whipped past the boat toward the prow.

"Pull up the forward anchor!" Bill was shouting at me because I was beside the rope. He fumed until it was safely inboard.

"Sure. Save that trout but kill your wife," I grunted, spreading my hands over the small of my back which felt as though a whale had slapped me with his tail. Bill didn't deign to reply for he was enraptured. His son was bringing in a rainbow! It was finning lazily beside the boat and I marveled that the fragile, almost invisible leader could have held him. After fishing for salmon, trout gear seemed dainty, and the fish so small. But now I realized that a fighting trout on a five-ounce rod and a cobweb leader was just as exciting as a salmon on a heavier setup.

Used to king salmon, I gazed in wonder at the pygmy rainbow flashing beside us. It wasn't much larger than the low-brow herring we used for salmon bait. But this was a little aristocrat! It had sheer filmy fins, scales delicate and jewel-toned. It rested for a moment, then flipped and darted down deep.

Bob played him well, unconscious of the shouts of encouragement from near-by fishermen. I admired the way he throttled his adolescent clumsiness and got the feel of that baby reel. He was winding it with thumb and forefinger while the remaining great big fingers stuck straight out in the manner of *nouveaux riches* holding teacups. With glazed eyes and open mouth, he was oblivious to the world. He elbowed his brother out of his way as he almost tenderly eased that trout to the surface. Now it was on its side and Cookie stood ready with the net.

I glanced apprehensively at Bill—this was risky business. If Cookie muffed the netting, there might be a

mass murder in the boat. However, before I had time to
worry further, Bob grabbed the net and brought that
trout in himself. Now our two gangling sons were beating each other on the back. Triumphantly, Bob un-
hooked the fish and held the beauty up for our approval.

"Mighty nice going, Bob. He'll run better than two
pounds. Bait up while I let the anchor out again." Then
Bill sprayed out a few more feed eggs with his slingshot
and let out his line. It hardly had sunk before we saw
him give it a sharp little tug. Then it shot out at a forty-
five-degree angle.

"Didn't I tell you Cascade is one of the best trout lakes
in Washington? Ought to be, the way it's stocked every
year. The scenery's just thrown in for good measure.
Say, look-at-that-little-devil-go, will you!"

It was racing around like a cat with a fit, only instead
of climbing curtains, it tried to slither under a log.
Cookie was so fascinated with the play he had forgotten
to bring his line in. Now he jumped when he felt it
jerk.

"Hey, Dad! I've got one too. What d'you know?
Must have set the hook by grabbing at it so hard."

"I'm certainly turning out to be the Evergreen fisherman," I grumbled, mad at every trout in the lake. "Everybody's hooked a fish except me."

Bill asked Bob to pull both anchors up and told
Cookie to work his trout around to the other side of the
boat. Bill was leaning forward, reeling in hard. Somebody hollered from a passing boat, "Watch it, Doc.
That's not a dogfish!"

Twice Bob started to hand the net to his father but
each time Bill shook his head. "Not yet. That trout
still has a trick or two up its sleeve." As he spoke, it

zipped out and ran under the boat. There was a mad scramble for places as Bill went forward in order to pass his rod over the bow of the boat. The rowboat rocked and we nearly shipped water, but the men wouldn't have noticed if Father Neptune, whiskers and all, had climbed right in beside me. Wholly intent, Bill played his fish and finally brought it in.

A few moments later Cookie got his. Crestfallen, he stared at it; anybody could see it lacked almost an inch of being the legal six-inch length.

"Back it goes. Too bad," Bill said.

"Please, Dad. It's almost big enough. Please!" But, firmly, Bill picked up the still quivering trout and slipped it back into the water, saying, "Nope. Good sportsmen stick to the rules. We'll come back and get him next year when he's fat and sassy. Right now, you'd have to get a baby-sitter for him. Bait up."

It was becoming very cold. The sun must have wearied of smiling down upon strong men fighting weak fish and turned its head away in disgust. While Bill was bringing in another trout, a silver this time, the first big raindrop splashed on my hand, a preview of the steady drizzle that set in. The sky fell down around our shoulders.

Bill just turned his collar up, jammed that hateful fishing hat lower, and said, "Now we'll really get 'em. Rainbows bite best in the rain." This sounded in character, but Bill didn't look right. He was nervous and his eyes had the tenseness I'd noticed just before he performed a serious operation. I was concerned, but there was such a hub-bub in the little-brown-jug boat that I turned to see what was happening. Both men were standing up and trying to struggle into slickers. The

boat was careening like a salmon ready for the net and
one man or the other was off balance most of the time.
The larger man couldn't turn his sleeve right side out
while his companion was in more serious difficulty. He
could not yank his raincoat off the floorboards though
he tried several times. With a vacant, foolish grin, he
said happily, "It'sh nailed down." When his friend sized
up the situation, he tottered forward and solemnly lifted
his buddy's foot off the slicker. The boat shipped water
and then it happened: a waving, sprawling body fell
overboard. There was a resounding splash and a moment later a head popped up beside the boat, the man's
hair plastered down like seaweed to a rock. A passing
troller leaned on his oars and went to the rescue, but he
had a tough time hoisting that sodden, jabbering man
over the transom. After his plunge, he was sober and,
amid cheers and jeers, he grabbed the oars and headed
for the main dock.

Bill said, "That, my sons, is a mixture of water and
alcohol, a solution not to be recommended."

The downpour never abated and I hoped the rainbows
were as ravenous as the rest of us. Bill landed five more
while the boys got several apiece. We fished another
hour and I never even had a nibble, or perhaps I was too
congealed to feel the line quiver. Cookie and Bob had
climbed into yellow oilskin slickers and knitted caps
which they took off every once in a while to wring the
water out of them. When I forgot and leaned my head
forward, a rivulet from the brim of my hat would trickle
down my neck. My legs were soaked and felt as though
they were encased in a layer of ice.

Finally I admitted to myself that I was still a fair-
weather fisherman—especially when I didn't get any fish.

Through chattering teeth, I blurted out, "Do you call this fun? Just tell me what you see in staying out here in this freezing rain!" I reeled in so fast the ratchet hummed in high "C," and slammed my rod down in the boat. "I'd rather have my appendix removed with a spoon than sit here any longer. Are those darn fool fish still biting?"

"No, as a matter of fact, they're not, my dear," said Bill, soothingly. "You stuck it out pretty well. It's after nine. We'll pull anchor and go in."

As we neared the dock, the noise and commotion increased. Dozens of men were standing around in the rain, gulping the hot coffee which was served on the dock and laughing and talking. I'd never seen so many teeth in my life. We waited in line for the game warden to inspect our fish for number, size, and possible tags. While he was weighing in our eighteen trout, a grinning prankster elbowed through the crowd, dragging a reluctant friend by the arm. "I tell you, Warden, he's got five silvers in his pockets. You better search him." There were smiles all around at the old gag.

Pushing through the crowd, we heard more familiar phrases about the big one that was "right up to the boat when—" One man was wagging his forefinger and saying to an amused group, "I'm not lying, boys, but that rainbow was so big—" Somebody good-naturedly clapped a hand over the speaker's mouth. Fishermen were peeking into creels and politely exclaiming over one another's catch. Rich and racy remarks ricocheted through the crowd, and of course Bill had to stop and gab with everyone he knew—while I stood there freezing in the rain. I thought any judge in the land would call this inhuman treatment or willful neglect and award

me a decree *and* the children. Or was this in the fine
print on the wedding license I had signed without reading? As I brooded I noticed the distinct smell of fried
fish over and above that of wet earth, rubber boots, and
mothballs. It was then I discovered the fishermen
bunched up in the park's community kitchen. At least
it would be dry, so I strolled over and saw men cleaning
fish, men frying fish on the big stove, and men talking
fish. It looked like a good setup but my heart wasn't
in it, so I found our car and got in. Soon Bill and the
boys joined me. My husband's spirits seemed to sag
with the starting of the car, and a heavy, ominous quiet
took over. Just to break the silence I asked, "Are we
taking the four-forty or the six o'clock ferry, Bill?"

"I don't know yet, dear. We'll see. Right now, as
soon as we get back to the cabin, we'll grab a bite and
all take naps. But we must be up by two, for we have
a most important appointment." With a sigh, he added,
"At least, I hope and pray it's going to be important
to us all."

I fumed because he wouldn't tell me what it was—but
you can't extract juice from a closed clam.

Bill shook us awake at one-thirty and the boys were
up with a bounce. Drat youth, I thought, stretching—
you never appreciate it until it's half gone. We got into
the car, Bill as mysterious as ever.

"Where we going, Dad?" Bob demanded.

"You'll soon see."

We saw—through the driving rain. For once I didn't
appreciate the beauty of newly washed ferns or sweep-
ing hemlock branches weighted down with water. We
drove through a grove of evergreens until we emerged

into a clearing where there were several cabins and an old farmhouse. I was surprised to see several cars parked near by. The occupants were standing on the edge of the bank, five men and four women. We left our car and walked toward them; even from this distance they looked vaguely familiar. Closer, I recognized Al Ul-brickson, the Washington crew coach. Why, there was Hazel, his wife! Wasn't that Louise Brookbank? And Doctor Brookbank?

"Say, what is this, Bill? A surprise party?"

"Perhaps. It also may be your future home."

"My what?"

"Just what I said, your summer home. That is," he added with the same worried abstraction I'd noticed for days, "if our friends want to go in with us and buy up this old resort. It's for sale and I've had a hell of a time rounding up congenial people who might be interested. And getting 'em here today; this rain—"

"Hi, Bill," said Wallie Hibbard, coming toward us and flipping water off the brim of his hat. I still was in a daze as I greeted his wife, Mabel, and met Mr. and Mrs. Kunde and Mr. Meyers. Everybody looked wet and unhappy—except Bill.

"Well, what do you think of it, folks?" Bill asked, waving his arm toward President's Channel that was dimpling in the rain. "It's the best salmon ground around here—right in your own front yard. We could tear down these cabins, clear a few trees, and—"

"How about a water supply?" Wallie's legal mind bit into essentials at once.

"Don't know. We'd have to find it. But look at that sandy beach! The Canadian mountains are right over there and—"

"How many acres, Bill?" Al Ulbrickson inquired.

"About thirty. Seven hundred feet of waterfront. If six families went in together, it wouldn't cost too much."

"It's wonderful," I breathed, just beginning to get the idea of the importance of this meeting. "Bill, I'd love a home in the San Juans more than anything else on earth."

"It looks god-forsaken to me," Hazel said. Mr. Meyers chimed in, "Water's scarce on these islands. Might cost a fortune to put in a good system and—"

"But look at that beach!" My heart was pounding so I could hardly talk. "Those cedars! And see that darling little point of land with the madrona tree on it. Just imagine having a home—"

"What would we do with the old farmhouse back there? It would cost a lot to tear it down—and all those other cabins?" Louise spoke thoughtfully, implying this was a fool's undertaking.

"Pull 'em down," Bill said easily. "You know, Al, there used to be a fish trap right out there." As he pointed westward, I noticed the clouds were parting. I'd been too befuddled to realize the rain had stopped. Cookie and Bob were hanging on their father's arm, begging and imploring him "to buy this beach."

"Dad, Dad, think of it! We could each have our very own boat!"

"I imagine the title of the property is all involved," Earl Brookbank said flatly. "It's nice but—I don't know." No one was particularly interested and I was sunk when the women started to walk toward their cars. I knew we couldn't swing such a big thing alone. Miserably, I listened while Bill told the men that the option on the place was up tomorrow, that it was now or never. Desperately I grasped Mr. Kunde's arm and said, "Can't you just see a salt-bleached cabin nestled under those cedars? Think of having your own boat at anchor out there. And how all of our children would love this beach."

But the group just stood around on one foot then the other.

"Well, I don't think we're interested," one of the men was drawling hesitantly when an amazing thing happened. It must have been a trick of the wind that parted the clouds so suddenly. One moment the world was gray, the next, bathed in sunshine! As the drab curtain was pulled aside, the snowy Canadian mountains swam into view and flakes of silver danced on each wave.

"Come back here," I yelled to the women.

"Look-at-that!" Mrs. Kunde said slowly, pointing to the vast expanse of water that glistened in the sunshine. As if to co-operate, the warmed cottonwood tree sent forth a most wonderful spicy fragrance. Louise Brookbank said it was one of the most beautiful views she'd ever seen. Now it was so warm we all opened our coats and spring thawed our spirits.

"You say there *are* fish right out here?" Mr. Kunde was beginning to melt. Bob was hugging me, whispering, "Mother, *make* Daddy buy, please." Dr. Brookbank looked toward the green-feathered slope of Turtleback Mountain a mile to our left and said carefully, "There *should* be water around here at the foot of that forest."

"See the alder thicket over yonder? That means water," Mabel was thinking out loud. Her husband added that he knew a lawyer who would untangle this reasonably.

"If we all went in together on a water system, perhaps it wouldn't cost so much," Wallie conceded.

"The price is not bad at all," Hazel said.

"Perhaps some Islander would tear these cabins down for nothing if he got the material in them," Louise said.

I just stood there, immobile, afraid to say anything lest I upset the delicate balance. In fact, no one spoke for a few moments, and in the contemplative quiet we could hear our boys shouting on the beach. They were racing around with young John Brookbank and Al Ulbrickson, junior, who were about their ages. I suggested we all walk along the shore, knowing it had persuasive powers greater than words. The four boys were already rigging up a raft out of driftwood logs and a piece of rope. Bill gazed at them with an indefinable look of longing on his face.

All at once, Wallie stopped skipping stones, Mabel left the log she had been sitting on, and the other women came toward us, excitement hastening their steps. But it was Wallie who slapped his fist in the flat of his other hand and said, "Let's grab it." One by one, everybody nodded assent. Then we all laughed, hugged one another, and jumped up and down in the sand.

"Hey, fellas!" Bill shouted to the boys. "D'you know you're playing on your very own beach?" With whoops and hollers they rushed up and fairly climbed all over him. When he could disentangle himself he pulled me aside and said, "Lord, but I'm relieved! I couldn't bear to tell you. I was so afraid the deal might not go through. And I couldn't have stood your disappointment on top of my own."

I looked at Bill in astonishment; men were simply incomprehensible. Any wife would rather share a disappointment than worry alone. But this was no time to tell him, for he was throwing out his arms and drinking in great chestfuls of salt air. Then he stooped down and picked up some sand. He poured it into my cupped fingers, saying, "It's ours, my dear. Every grain of it." His words were slow and drawn out to prolong the ecstasy in their meaning.

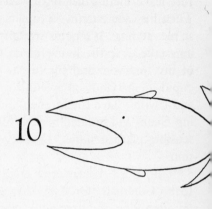

10

Till fish us do part

During the following week, we were in a constant tizzy—all except Bill. And he had to pinch himself to maintain his professional calm. Every evening we gathered around the dining room table and drew highly individualized plans for our new home on Orcas. Cookie wanted a bedroom large enough to build a boat in while Bob's numerous sketches included a lean-to with fifteen bunks, "so I can have all the fellas at once." I wanted a Swedish peasant house but Bill thought I was crazy.

"What's the idea of a Scandahoovian house?" he demanded. "I suppose you want grass on the roof and a billy goat to mow it. But go ahead if you want to.

Just leave me a great big closet for my fishing tackle."
Then his eyes narrowed to slits and he shook his finger
at me, adding, "Get this straight. You can let the Vik-
ings take over the living room but you keep them out
of my bedroom and the kitchen. I don't want any fat
cupids or garlands of Swedish roses painted in my room
and I won't have the kitchen all cluttered up with rocking chairs and braided garlic. Get it? Now look at this
sensible plan of mine. Don't you like the front eleva-
tion?"

"I do not," I answered emphatically. "What is it—
Idaho Colonial? Or Early Iowa? Now look, Bill, how
do you like my fireplace?" Surprisingly enough, we
agreed upon a huge floor-to-ceiling job to be made of
sandstone blocks from Sucia Island.

The next Friday night, the Hibbards, the Ulbricksons,
and the Brookbanks met us on the ferry. We were going to the Island to decide upon a water supply. Cookie
and Bob were with us, for the boys and I were staying
on the following week as it was their spring vacation.
Bill had to return Sunday evening with the others, but
he promised he would come back the minute he could
and bring our new fishing boat with him.

We all took cabins at the West Beach Resort near
our property and talked far into the night: the men,
about drilling a well versus tapping a spring; Hazel,
Louise, Mabel and I, about far more important things
such as where to buy the best glazed chintz and the gay-
est color for window boxes.

After breakfast the next morning, we all linked arms
and walked up the beach to our land. I didn't see how
the men could keep their minds on a water system when
the wide, sandy shore was so enticing. What was the

diameter of a water pipe when the firs on the bank were just breaking out those jade green, new-growth tassels? Tiny unfurled maple leaves were cupped and tender as a baby's hand. Everywhere were the wondrous signs of spring. April was fairly bursting her seams—and so were we.

While the others went up the fern-bordered path from the beach, I stopped for a lingering glance at President's Channel, awash in a dozen shades of blue. About two miles straight across from us lay Waldron Island, and there was Ethan Allen's cove shimmering in the sunshine. The Canadian mountains still were hidden under their nightcap of clouds.

I ran to join the group. Al Ulbrickson was saying something about a spring on Turtleback Mountain.

"Why not try our own alder grove first?" Wallie Hibbard said. "Alders mean water. What d'you think, Bill?"

For some reason, my husband colored and looked most uncomfortable. He ran his fingers through his hair and stammered, "I thought it was a good idea—I mean, it won't cost much to— Oh, hell, what I'm trying to say is that I've hired a water witch to go over the place. You know, a dowser. He's due here right now."

"You mean one of those guys who claims he can locate water with a forked willow stick?" Earl Brookbank looked at Bill in amazement and then laughed with the rest of us. Al Ulbrickson, the graduate engineer, just chuckled, but Wallie spouted, "Do you believe in that rot, Bill? Anybody with a scientific mind knows it's pure bunk." He clapped Bill on the shoulder and grinned at him, adding, "I'll not take any more of your pills, Doc. Bet you roll 'em yourself by the dark of the moon and make them out of powdered frogs and snakes' whiskers."

He stopped kidding when we saw a man approach—a normal-looking, middle-aged man without a suggestion of witch about him. But he was it—the dowser. After introductions, we women walked behind the men so we could enjoy our amusement unseen.

As we approached the grove, Mabel nudged me and said, "Don't you worry about your boys, Bea, even if Bill does believe in witches. Maybe they're throwbacks and will turn out perfectly normal." There was no time to answer, for our husbands were calling us to watch the witch cut a willow wand. From a limb where two branches joined to form a "Y," he cut the pronged stick that was about two feet long. Then he gripped each fork hard and held it in front of him, parallel to the ground. As he walked back and forth, he was the only person who didn't have a silly smirk on his face.

He was pushing through the undergrowth of ferns and salal when he suddenly stopped. We saw that forked wand bending toward the ground.

"He's twisting it in his hands," I whispered to Hazel. Now the dowser stepped back a few paces and then forward again to cover the same ground. In exactly the identical spot, the wand dipped as it had before. We watched him intently, but his hands did not move when the stick bent earthward.

"Fine," Wallie was saying in his best legal manner. "So we have water right here." He rubbed his hands together and winked at Bill.

"Yep, you do," the witch replied calmly. He handed his stick to Earl, saying, "You men might try. Never know who has the gift." Earl, Bill, and Al took turns, but the wand never moved as they passed it over the indicated spot. Wallie shook his head when it was handed to him but the dowser insisted, so, with a brave effort at being a good sport, he went through the procedure. The rest of us had turned and started to walk away when he let out a yell.

"Hey! Look!" We all whirled around in time to see the willow branch bend toward the earth.

"My God," he said, a blank look on his face, "watch that stick!" His knuckles stood out with strain as he clutched the prongs of the wand. Backing off, he tried it again and again. Each time the stick was pulled toward the ground. There was no doubt about it. No one spoke. Then Wallie flung the branch away as though it had bitten him. With glazed eyes he kept murmuring, "I tell you, it did move. It did." He really was unnerved.

" 'Tain't nuthin' to be so upset about," the dowser comforted. "You're jest a natural-born witch, that's all."

While the men were telling the dowser to go ahead and dig the well, I turned to Mabel and said, "Now, dear, about *your* child. Don't you worry. She resembles your side of the family."

Just then Cookie and Bob came tearing up, shouting that there was a man to see us and that he'd been waiting a long time.

"Must be Ray Pineo," Bill said. "He's going to do our building." We both went over to talk to him and immediately liked this shy man with his engaging smile and great serious blue eyes. We paced off the building site and talked about the plans all afternoon, and by evening we knew our beloved home was in the best of hands.

Bill returned with the others the following day, but Cookie and Bob and I stayed on at the resort cabin. It was a deliriously happy week. Ray Pineo brought two axes and taught the boys how to fell the few trees we must sacrifice. I didn't mind losing the firs growing right on the building site, and shivers of excitement chased up my back as I watched our two husky sons clear the land. But it hurt to part with that glorious shaggy-barked cedar growing on the bank in front of the house. I couldn't bear to see the boys' axes bite into that living wood. When it fell, I stopped my ears against its splintering shriek; the death agony of a great tree is a terrible thing to witness. However, with those lacy branches gone, our magnificent panorama shone through the clearing and I drank in the view that was to keep me company for so many years. If it is true that one owns all his heart and spirit can encompass, then half of President's Channel, those rugged, rocky headlands on Kimple's Point, and all of the Canadian Selkirk Mountains belong to me.

Thursday morning, we got up early and tore through breakfast, though there wasn't any sense in our haste. Bill couldn't possibly arrive until the noon ferry, but our enthusiasm had to be worked off some way. He had written that he was not only bringing our sixteen-foot outboard motorboat but also *two* surprises. Just how he was going to get that boat off the ferry and into the water, I couldn't imagine. But he would.

While we flew around cleaning up the cabin, we all tried to think of a name for it.

"It should pertain to fish," I mused aloud.

"Or lack of fish," Cookie twinkled. We mentioned dozens of possible names but none clicked. Then Bob clapped his hands and shouted, "I've got it! You know how we don't always get fish, Mother. Let's call it the *Nun-Yet*."

"That's it!" Cookie yelled and pounded his brother on the shoulder until Bob gave him a mild, protective left-to-the-jaw. And so our boat was named before we had even seen it.

By eleven-thirty we were on the tip-end of the dock. The ferry was only a toy in the distance. We were nearly crazy with speculation, wondering what the surprises could be. That ferry took forever to come in, but finally we saw Bill on the car deck waving to us. The dog barked and the boys yelled as the boat stuck her rounded nose between the pilings. There was the *Nun-Yet!*

Now Bill was talking to deck hands, but the boys, past coherent speech, just jumped up and down. The moment the ferry docked, Cookie and Bob pushed through the stream of passengers and cars and helped lower *Nun-Yet* from the deck into the water. Bob jumped in and Bill handed him down the oars, and a minute later, a brand-new ten-horsepower outboard motor. As if that wasn't exciting enough, he turned and helped the deck hands launch another boat, a tiny, clinker-built dinghy! Inside this sturdy little eight-foot boat were leaboards and a rudder. Cookie jumped into it and he nearly exploded when his father handed down a mast and a snow-white sail.

The *Nun-Yet's* maiden voyage was a huge success; she fairly breezed through the element for which she had been so well designed. Her prow sliced the water as proudly as any fifty-footer, but our love was divided between her and the appealing dinghy-sailboat. It towed beautifully and touched the water as lightly as a herring gull.

While we were proceeding through narrow Pole Pass, Bill calmed down enough to tell us how he had bought the dinghy second-hand. It had come off a Canadian yacht, and an old sea captain he knew had rigged up the removable sailing equipment and repainted the stout oak frames and cedar siding. Now, even with the indignity of being towed, she rode the waves so majestically that Cookie found a name for her.

"She's English, Dad—and about the handsomest boat in the world. White, too. Just for fun, let's call her *Queen Mary*."

An hour later, it was *Queen Mary* which took us ashore, two at a time. *Nun-Yet* rode at anchor in front of our rented cabin. While Bill tore into his old clothes, he kept peeking out the window, admiring our boat. He wore his fifty-dollar smile.

"That's sure sixteen feet of marine splendor," he said, with a pouter-pigeon swell to his chest. "What do you say we zip over to Waldron Island this afternoon? Perhaps the herring are through spawning in East Sound and West Sound and have returned to their grounds off Point Disney. I always get them there in summer but I've never tried in the spring. Want to?"

"Yes—but what would you do with a mess of herring now? There isn't a silver within fifty miles of here and the kings haven't come in yet."

"I know, but there's another reason. I'd like to take a bucket of herring over to Nestor Nordstrom to preserve for me. He has a trick formula that makes 'em swell bait. They stay shiny and are lots tougher. I might want some in a hurry this summer."

"Tennie," our new ten-horsepower motor, did her stuff, and we zipped over to the southern tip of Waldron Island, past the point, and into Cowlitz Bay. When we were lined up with Sandy Point and the old rock quarry on Orcas Island and straight out from the dock on Waldron, Bill cut the motor.

"Now," he said, "if they've finished their courting, they should be here. That is, if the winter run of kings haven't gobbled 'em all up while they were spawning on the eel grass in those protected bays. Hand me that board, please."

The six-foot-long, ten-pound-test, gut herring gig was wound around a board so that the eight hooks on their short drop lines wouldn't get tangled together. But those were the oddest steelhead hooks I'd ever seen. They were pure white.

"Where'd you get white hooks, Bill? What's the idea? Are you using white for the herring brides just returning from their honeymoons?"

"Hardly. Most of 'em are old married women by now. You know, herring spawn again and again. No, this is Ben White's idea and he's one of the hottest guides on Orcas. He said there was no use throwing hooks away after they started to rust—as they do in just a few weeks. He dips them in white marine paint. He says herring like white hooks even better than silver. Ben claims they are more alluring than those with bits of colored yarn tied to the shank like they use in British Columbia. Well, we'll give 'em a whirl."

He unwound a second gigging outfit and tied eight-ounce sinkers on the ends of both lines, then fastened the other ends to cuttyhunk lines on regulation star drag reels. He used our long, limber spinning poles. I was thinking that the trout fisherman had nothing on us. He may chase flies or bugs for future bait. We chased herring.

Bill handed a rod to each boy, saying, "They must be here. See all those Great Northern loons working around us? This incoming tide should boil the herring to the surface. All set?"

He told them to keep their thumbs pressed tightly on the line wound on the reel and then flip off the brake. When about ten feet had plunged out, he showed them how to gig their rods up sharply several times and let the spring of the pole flip the lines so that the hooks below would flutter on their drop lines.

"Feel anything? Does the line quiver at all?" The boys solemnly shook their heads.

"Well, let out another ten feet and repeat the gigging. You never know at what depth you'll find 'em. At Point Lawrence I've hit herring just under the surface and, then again, twenty or thirty feet down. When you strike bottom, bring your line in just as you let it out, gigging every ten feet on the way up." They tried it several times before Cookie said seriously, "Something's-playing-around-with-my-hooks." Then with a big grin he began to reel in fast.

"Hey. Quit it," Bill snapped. "Don't bring it in yet. Just keep it moving gently and give the herring time to take the other hooks. That's it. Now haul her in quickly. But don't jerk." Hanging over the side of the boat, we all saw four herring swirl to the surface as the line came in.

"Hold your rod straight up," Bill said as he swung the gig line inboard. The herring glinted and flapped over our heads. He told Cookie to take the fish off the hooks carefully so they would live longer in the tub of sea water we had stowed under the prow. As he un-hooked the last herring and slithered it into the tub, Bob swung his gig line over the boat. He was as excited as a fox terrier, for all his eight hooks had herring.

"Full house!" his father exclaimed. "You've got the hang of it." But the next few attempts netted no fish, for we had been carried off the hot spot by the tide. So Bill started the motor, but even when we were over it again, we got nothing.

"Often happens. Soon as the tide levels off a bit, they quit. And sometimes they stop biting just to be ornery. That's why you should let out line in ten-foot jumps. They don't bite very long at a time and when they are hitting, you want to find the depth where they are quickly and not fool around. Well, gigging is over. How'd you like to tempt a king with these herring? If we should snag one on these limber spinning poles, we'd have our hands full." He glanced at me and added, "Don't look so doubtful. A lot of kings just hang around the Sound and don't ever go to sea. Pessimistic fishermen get gastric ulcers. Hand me my tackle box."

"It's silly enough to fish in April, but you are sure to be skunked now. Look over there!" He squinted in the direction of my finger at the tall black fin that was knifing through the water a few hundred yards away. It was a killer-whale, often called blackfish. Behind it, a cow's shorter dorsal fin could be seen. These junior-grade whales are twenty to thirty feet long and drive salmon crazy.

"Um, mebbe it's just a happy couple that have skipped school. If there are only a few of them, the salmon won't leave." He was putting an eight-inch live herring on the setup, inserting the lead hook up through the jaw, and fixing the two triple hooks on either side of the fish. He looked at it critically and said, "If we run into blackmouth which are young kings, these gang hooks may be a trifle too large. I'll change to a smaller size if we get strikes but lose too many fish. That sometimes helps. Will I fix you a herring, too?"

"No, thank you," I said loftily. "I've got a hunch the salmon may be feeding on the small, three-inch herring, so I'm going to cut myself a spinner. And I want a double-ought, half-and-half flasher." Bill smiled. A lot of water had gone under the Deception Pass bridge since I started fishing. Now I called my shots. I was no longer a novice—but I chose a thoroughly dead herring to fillet into my beveled-edge, pennant-shaped spinner.

Bill had trouble cutting the big motor to proper trolling speed but he finally did it, grumbling that our spark plugs soon would be fouled. I pulled out eighty feet of line, using the flat of my hand as much as I could so as not to kink the soft wire line. My spinner had whirled a little as I tried it, but I knew it would calm down into the desired swimming-darting motion under the pressure of water at trolling depth.

Now both our lines were out and my rod's tip had a nice steady little tick, like a heartbeat, so I knew my flasher was swashing sideways as it should. If we had been going too fast and the flasher was whirling, my rod would have shimmied. Bill read my thoughts and said, "You're right. Nine-tenths of Fisherman's Luck lies in knowing which lure to use when and how to adjust the trolling speed so as to get the best action from it. The other tenth is knowing where the fish are."

We had been trolling along a slick, copper-colored

ribbon of water outlined by a tide-rip's frothy edge. Now Bill tried zigzagging across it, saying this was what Bud Kimple did. And Bud always got fish.

"Hooray for Bud! I've got a strike!" No one believed me, for it was an easy one and I didn't know the score myself until I felt that second bang.

"Cut the motor," I yelled, holding my voice down to a well-bred holler. I had a king—and six hundred feet of line. I was ready for him. I wasn't a bit surprised at his three-hundred-foot run and the terrific jerks he gave at the end of it. Then one instant the line was throbbing —and the next, it fell slack. That salmon was dashing toward the boat, not fighting a bit.

Bill was enjoying himself. He drawled, "Betcha it's not a king at all. Probably it's a *lutefisk* that just got wind of your Swedish house." When it was nearly in, the line snapped taut, and after a leisurely run, that king started sulking and logging down like the big thirty-pounders do. Yet I knew from the feel of the line he was a small king. There was something odd about the whole business. Suddenly he started to run and the ratchet hummed in a steady monotone. Cookie was cheering me on, yelling, "Mom's on the beam—cooking on all four burners." Again the line came in too easily and now I could see the shine of my leader. Then we saw the salmon, a long, quiet form. It was curiously spent and wasn't moving, yet the water around it was churning white.

"Look!" Bob was at my elbow, pointing down to the huge dogfish that was thrashing under the king. It darted up and I could see the leering to-hell-with-you look in those emerald green eyes.

"Steady as she goes," Bill was chanting. "Keep his

head up but be ready for a run. Cookie, you're going to gaff this one." I was proud of the boy. He did a good job though he got the gaff hook in the belly and not under a gill, as experts do. But it stayed on the hook when he hauled it overside. As it slapped to the floorboards, we all gasped at once. For there was a long, deep, bleeding gash on one side.

"Hum," Bill said, "no wonder he came in so fast that first time. Looks like a seal made a real pass at him."

"Was that dogfish trying to nab him, too?" Bob asked.

"No. It just smelled the blood and followed him to the surface. Even a big doggie wouldn't attack a healthy king of this size. Kind of think this will run twelve or fourteen pounds."

I said, "Well, it's my fish, I caught it—and I get to clean it." We all laughed for, long ago, the boys had discovered our hoax and now never fought for the so-called "privilege" of cleaning fish.

In early spring around these islands, a day may be most ladylike and then, with no apparent provocation, turn into a hellion. The wind was beginning to freshen and we both knew we should run for home. We stowed our gear and Bill tried to start the motor, but it coughed like a sea lion and then snarled at him.

"Dirty plugs, Dad. Let me clean them," Bob said. We both looked at him in amazement, wondering where he had picked up all this information. Bill tried the engine one more time, without success, then Bob cleaned the plugs.

His hands still were smeared with oil and carbon when we sat down to a baked salmon dinner several hours later. This was no garden-run baked fish; this was strictly blue-ribbon stuff. May Gerard, one of my new

island friends, had told me how to cut the fillet salmon
into serving-sized chunks and place them skin-side down
in a baking pan. Then, it was just a simple matter of salt,
pepper, a little lemon juice and about a pint of thick
sour cream. During the hour it bakes, something mysterious happens—the salmon flakes up and forgets to taste
fishy at all and the cream turns into a tart, delicious
sauce. The only complaint we had was that it was so
rich that we couldn't eat more than three or four serv-
ings. But those were unbelievably good. It may have
been that last big chunk which made me restless during
the night, for I dreamed it was June and we were moving into our new home on Orcas.

Ten weeks later, that dream came true. June had
dragged its heels, but we all had been busy enough,
painting and building furniture. Bill had wrinkled up his
nose in disgust at the birds and bright red hearts I had
painted on turquoise chairs. "Do the Swedes like that
stuff? Thought they were fishermen. Why don't you
put on a couple of salmon with a herring border? Or a
bunch of shamrocks for the glory of the family tree?"
But he really liked them.

Two days before we left, we sent up a truckload of
furniture, a lot of it early Sears, Roebuck garnered from
friends' attics, but the mattresses were new and good.
Maybe some fishermen don't mind sleeping on hard beds.
I do.

On Wednesday, June 30th, Bill backed my car out of
the garage and hitched "Fanny" on the rear bumper.
This was the name we had given our trailer for we always had so much behind. Now we loaded it down.
On top of the pile in the back seat of the car we made
room for Bonnie who had been barking to go for an

hour. Our lovely gray Persian cat, Eleanor, the traveler, had to go, too. It was unfortunate that she had recently presented us with kittens whose dependability on a trip was as doubtful as their paternity. But Cookie fixed up a portable sand box. It was nobody's fault that it later turned over en route.

After I had packed last-minute things, I looked around the living room to be sure nothing was forgotten. Of course I ran into Hannah's frown. It seemed to me she never had approved of this Orcas home at all. Splendidly ensconced in her gold-leaf frame, she had been reminding me for weeks—rather hypocritically, I thought—that "Willful waste makes woeful want." She had something there all right, but then her husband hadn't been Irish and she had never been convinced by a play named, *You Can't Take It With You.* Fervently, I wished she had, for she might have been pleasanter to live with if all her epigrams weren't so dreary. Poor old Pinch-penny continued to scowl as I blew her a farewell kiss and went happily out the door.

I climbed into the car and took my place behind the wheel. Bill wasn't going with us. He had several patients he couldn't leave, but he hoped to come up for the week end. He kissed me and reached over the yowling cat to kiss the boys, muttering something about being glad he wasn't traveling with a zoo. Eleanor didn't approve of moving a maternity ward.

Neither did I as those eighty long miles stretched out, but I comforted myself with the thought of crisp, cool sheets on my new bed that night. And how much fun it would be to arrange the furniture tomorrow. I hoped the paint in the bedrooms was dry for I wanted to get the curtains up. It probably was, for Ray Pineo had

promised to put on a big crew and have the house ready
by the last of June.

I was dead tired by the time I had that swaying trailer
and the car parked on the ferry, and we were so eager
to get there that the trip seemed to last a hundred years.
Purposely, we didn't have dinner on the ferry; it would
be so thrilling to have it in our new home. Wouldn't
take a jiffy to get the wood stove roaring and—

"Mother!" Bob rushed to me in tears. It seemed
Eleanor had jumped out of the car and now, half crazy,
was tearing around under all the automobiles on deck.
I had visions of doing her homework and raising her
babies with a medicine dropper, but Cookie finally cap-
tured her with a blanket just as the cars were rolling off
at the Orcas ferry slip.

Poor Fanny never had such a bumpy ride as we tore
over the country roads. Impatience to see our new
home kept my foot close to the floorboard. At last we
turned into our own lane, and there stood our house. A
house without a roof! My jaw dropped in unbelieving
dismay, which grew as we noted that it also was innocent of doors and windows. Dumbfounded, I just stared
at this shell of a house. Then, with pricked-bubble
spirits, we started toward it, stumbling over piles of
lumber and sewer pipes to the kitchen. The stove was
there all right, but the sink was resting on it. It was
filled with coils of wire, carpenter tools, and an electric
saw. The stovepipe had been put in the oven, evidently
for safekeeping.

The living room was a sight to behold: all the furniture
was stacked in one corner, mattresses on top. I sank
down on a keg of nails and tried to swallow my disappointment. As children will, Bob and Cookie rose to

the situation and put their arms around me, saying *they* would get dinner. I heard them fussing around outside, but I still was in a daze as I climbed up the ladder to my "bedroom." Only naked two-by-fours marked it off from the rest of the rooms and the evening sky shone down through the rafters.

Now the boys were calling me and I went outside to find a nice bonfire going in a safely cleared place near the house.

"Sit here, Mother," Cookie directed as he pulled a can of beans from the fire and dumped the contents on three shingles. Bob had pared another shingle into strips we used for forks and he'd even found a can of dog food for Bonnie. Somehow that dinner prepared by our sons took the sting out of my disappointment. I glowed over their self-reliance, picked up, no doubt, from our many fishing trips. Bob and the motor, Cookie's interest in building a boat, and their good sportsmanship on rugged trips gave them a "savvy" which only comes from growing up in a fisherman's family.

It was dark by the time we put the fire out and by flashlight I tucked Eleanor and her brood into a safe corner with a fresh box of sand close by. I gave her a mother-to-mother talk about the importance of training children young. Then we hauled the mattresses off onto the floor and rolled up in blankets. The tears I shed on the dog's neck were due more to exhaustion than anything else.

We were awakened next morning by the carpenters coming to work. Understandably enough, they weren't a bit pleased to see us, and Ray said unhappily, "Guess I should have let you know. We ran into trouble getting supplies from the mainland. But I'll get the stove hooked up right now."

While we had breakfast on the beach it came to me that I must never let the Island tempo upset me. The relaxing, leisurely pace had soothed my heart and nerves so many times that now it would be ungrateful to bite the hand that fed me. Anyway, Bill would be up in two days and then, magically, everything would be all right.

City carpenters would have quit a job where they had to build a house around a family. We must have been dreadfully in the way, but the men didn't show their irritation; they did everything they could to make us as comfortable as possible and I warmed to the ways of the Islanders who genuinely enjoy helping others. We were such a bother that I certainly didn't blame them for having some fun at my expense. I was all innocence when Ray Pineo handed me a five-gallon oil tin and said, "We're going to install the septic tank today and I want you to go to Templin's store and get some septic tank starter, will you?" I should have noticed his twisted grin and the way all the other carpenters were hanging around, smiling. But I didn't.

When I found Karl, he was in his long white coat, slicing bacon. I told him what I wanted and handed him the can. He bent over double, laughing, and called the other clerks. Between chuckles, he said, "Ray's pulled it again. On another greenhorn." More giggling, and then Karl took me aside while he explained, with hesitating delicacy, what really starts the microbiologic action in a septic tank. I returned with an empty can—an amused and wiser woman.

Every time I turned around for the next two days, I wished Bill were there. There was so much to do. The future garden should be spaded, a float made for the *Nun-Yet*, a shack built on the beach to store motors and tackle. The boys were having a grand time helping shingle the house, but all I could do was run around in meaningless circles. After a day or so, life without a sink, doors, windows, or roof gets a trifle thick, especially when there is nothing to prevent sea gulls from roosting on the toilet.

But Saturday finally came and Bill was coming up on the early boat. By ten o'clock the boys were watching the road, and when I heard Turtleback Mountain echo with yips and yells, I ran out to meet my husband. Of course I'd written him about the few drawbacks of our homecoming, but the lack of windows and walls didn't bother him a bit. In a glow, he wandered about the house, delighted to find his fishing gear safely stowed in the place that was going to be his tackle closet. But every time I'd suggest he spade the garden, he found some excuse to go to the beach, and once he yelled up to me, "Hey, look at those herring boil right in your front yard."

I suggested we have lunch on the beach, but Bill squared his shoulders, beat his breast, and said, "A man's place is in his own home." So we ate sitting on stumps where the porch was going to be. That is, between jumps, for every few minutes Bill popped up to point at the widening ring in the water where a salmon had just rolled. I was happy as could be, and we decided we must be two reincarnated souls of fishermen who had died of frustration in the Middle West and been reborn in Paradise.

We were startled to hear a car stop in the driveway. A moment later, Cappy Bell sauntered toward us and

Bill rushed to meet his old friend. "Well, well, Cappy. Mighty good to see you. How'd you know I was on the Island? Come on, Cappy, see our new house." Bill clapped his arm around Cappy's shoulder and the old man's hard-bitten face cracked wide open in a smile. For a fleeting moment, his sharp blue eyes held the same tenderness I'd often seen in Bill's when he looked at his own sons. Then, abruptly, he snapped back into character, brushed his hand under his nose, and spit in a pile of shavings.

Bill took him into the huge living room and Cappy looked about, critically. Then he sniffed and said, "Gaffed yourself quite a house, didn't yuh, Bill?"

"Glad you like it," Bill said, expansively, thumbs slipped under his suspenders. "But I have to be fair about it. Most of the ideas are Bea's."

"Thought so," the old man grunted, still paying me no attention. Man-like, Bill was oblivious to Cappy's subtle disapproval. With or without a roof, a lady should be courteous in her own home, so I asked Cappy to sit down, indicating a barrel which would place him in a strong draft. His sly look belied his words when he said quickly, "Nope. I just came to see the house." They poked around for quite a while and then returned to the living room. Cappy was silent.

"Well, d'you like it?" Bill asked complacently.

"Hell no. I tell yuh, Bill, she's takin' yuh. You don't need a layout like this to git fish. Why cut a leg off to git a splinter out of your toe?" Bill saw my feathers begin to ruffle and quickly shoved Cappy out the door, saying, "Come on down to the beach and see the boats. This way."

When they returned, Cappy pushed his duck-bill cap

on the back of his head, thoughtfully scratched his ear with his thumb, and said, "I like them boats. See yuh heve some sense. But—" he gestured around the room— "I oughta warn yuh, Bill. They say eels soon git used to bein' skinned. Watch it. Now, how about *me* and *you* taking a little run over to Waldron this afternoon? Got my blankets in case we tie into 'em." Then a tense, expectant expression came over his face and he whispered audibly, "Hey, Bill, where's your used-beer department?"

Just then, Ray Pineo called to me from upstairs—or rather, up the ladder. He wanted to know where I wanted a linen closet. We talked it over for quite a time before we decided. Then, above the noise of hammering, I thought I heard the putt-putt of an outboard motor. I descended that shaky ladder two rungs at a time and ran to the opening left for the front door.

Nun-Yet, with her nose pointed mid-channel, was leaving a rippling wake behind her. Cappy and Bill sat on either side of the motor, their heads together.

Nailed to the door frame beside me, a note fluttered in the breeze. It read:

> Darling, I love you, I love the children, and I love our new house. But I had to go fishing with Cappy.
>
> Yours—till fish us do part
> Bill.